JavaScript Async

Events, Callbacks, Promises and Async Await

Ian Elliot

I/O Press
I Programmer Library

ISBN Paperback: 978-1871962567

First Edition
First Printing November, 2017
Revision 0

Published by IO Press   www.iopress.info
in association with I Programmer   www.i-programmer.info

The publisher recognizes and respects all marks used by companies and manufacturers as a means to distinguish their products. All brand names and product names mentioned in this book are trade marks or service marks of their respective companies and our omission of trade marks is not an attempt to infringe on the property of others.

Preface

Asynchronous programming is essential to the modern web and at last JavaScript programmers have the tools to do the job – the Promise object and the async and await commands. These are so elegant in their design that you need to know about them if only to be impressed. It is likely that other languages will incorporate similar facilities in the future.

While async and await make asynchronous code as easy to use as synchronous code – who said synchronous code was easy! In fact there are still a lot of subtle things going on when you use async and await and to really master the situation you need to know about Promises and you need to know about how the JavaScript dispatch queue works. It seems like a lot, but once you do understand it you can mostly just get on with coding. It is when things don't work as you expect that the deeper knowledge can surface and help you sort out what is happening.

Finally is it "asynchronous" or is it "async"?

I have used both and swapped from one to the other as it seemed to fit in with the sentence in question. I hope this doesn't upset any readers, but sometimes the full "asynchronous" seems just right and in others the more casual "async" seems "righter".

I'd like to thank Kay Ewbank and Sue Gee for their input in proof reading the manuscript. As with all book length endeavors, there are still likely to be mistakes, hopefully few in number, which are entirely mine.

This book is a heavily revised and updated version of a series which first appeared on the I Programmer website, www.i-programmer.info.

To keep informed about forthcoming titles visit the publisher's website:
www.iopress.info
This is where you will find errata and update information.
You can also provide feedback to help improve future editions.

Table of Contents

Chapter 10
Fetch, Cache and ServiceWorker 139

Chapter 1
Modern JavaScript and Async

Asynchronous programming is what most of us have to work with. It is therefore surprising that even a language like JavaScript, that was created to work with asynchronous events, has only very recently gained the facilities it needs to make async easier. In this book we examine the basic ideas of async programming, what it is, why it is needed, and how we can organize code to create programs that behave well in an async environment.

Modern JavaScript?

The first problem in using JavaScript today is which versions of JavaScript you can rely on. JavaScript stagnated for a long time, but now we are seeing an update every year. The stagnation of JavaScript was a shame, but it has provided a very dependable core for the language that you can mostly rely on. Of course JavaScript has been standardized as ECMAScript, but the original name lives on.

The long lived version was ES3, which was the standard for ten years from around 1999 to 2009 when ES5 started to be widely adopted. Today the features of ES6 are available to 80% or more of browser users because of the way that browsers are updated online. This book is about many of the new features in ES6 and later, but it is also about how ES3 and ES5 deal with the same problems.

The reason for this looking back is two-fold. The first reason is that to completely understand some of the modern ways of doing things you need to know what they are based upon. So ES6 makes use of the Promise and ES 2007 introduced async and await as ways of dealing with asynchronous code. However, async and await are based on the use of the Promise and many functions in JavaScript continue to use the original callback method. To master the stack you need to know the original ways of doing things and the best way we have today.

You will also discover that most of the examples in this book do not use the most up-to-date possible JavaScript. The reason for this is that when you are trying to master some new feature it can be difficult to know what is essential to the new feature. For example, using Promises with arrow functions might give the impression that arrow functions are somehow an essential component of the Promise. Of course, they aren't.

9

In most cases the simplest example that makes the case for the new feature is the best, even if it fails to make use of all the other possible new features.

Of course, when you are writing real code you will often find that the best code does make use of all of the new JavaScript features, but it helps to be aware that this is not always the case.

Can I Use?

With any new feature, one of the most difficult decisions is to use it or not. If you use it then your code is better and perhaps you can deliver a better experience to your end users. Of course, the downside is that your code will not run on earlier implementations of JavaScript and this generally means earlier browsers.

In general Internet Explorer (IE) is the biggest problem as it is no longer being developed by Microsoft and it is still used on older versions of Windows – especially servers. Older legacy browsers are used by only a relatively small percentage of machines, but they might be important percentages in some cases. The most significant being the 4% or so who are still using IE. The good news is that nearly all of them, about 3%, are using IE 11 which does support many of the more advanced features.

Of the modern browsers, Microsoft's Edge and Apple's Safari are also usually problematic. In the case of Edge it is because it is a relatively new browser and its development team are struggling to implement all of the old and new features that a modern browser should support. In the case of Apple it is mostly a matter of having a closed ecosystem which means that it is possible to pick and choose features which fit in with Apple's approach to software. In some cases Safari is ahead of the pack, and in other cases it drags its feet until the feature is so obviously successful and required that not to implement it would be a disadvantage.

To find out which browsers support what features, the best advice is to use caniuse.com and type in the name of the feature you are interested in. From this you can discover which browser versions support it and get an estimate of the percentage support.

For example, at the time of writing, Can I Use shows that nearly all current browsers support the Promise object with the obvious exception of IE 11 and Opera Mini. It also shows a better than 89% support.

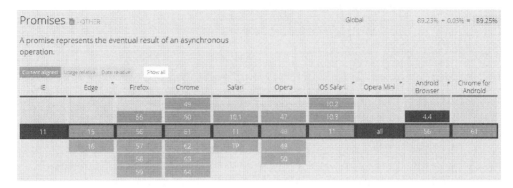

You can make use of "Can I Use" to make estimates of the percentage of people that your use of a feature will make your code unusable for.

Employing Polyfills

If you can't afford to lose a slice of your audience the simplest solution is just not to use the unsupported feature. There is usually a way of using ES5 to achieve the same result.

A popular alternative to this is to seek out and use a polyfill. JavaScript, even early versions, is a capable language and it is usually possible to find a way to provide the same facility. For example, there are a number of JavaScript polyfill libraries that will give you essentially the Promise object, even if the version of JavaScript you are using doesn't support it.

The big problem with polyfill libraries is that they are rarely as good as the fully implemented feature. They often are only partial implementations and even full implementations tend to have restrictions and differences.

There is one polyfill that takes a different approach. Babel is essentially a compiler that takes the most up-to-date version of JavaScript as its input and outputs ES5 which works on most browsers. The main downside of this approach is that you have to use a compiler and you almost certainly will not recognize the JavaScript that is produced.

Browsers and Node.js

All of the code in this book has been tested with the latest versions of Chrome and Firefox which are 61 and 56. All of the code should work on all modern browsers with the exception of the Service Worker API in Chapter 9, which is currently not implemented on Edge or Safari.

The browser is the environment considered as standard, but everything discussed will work with Node.js where it makes sense. There is of course no DOM in Node.js and no UI. Node.js is based on Chrome's V8 JavaScript engine and has all of the language features that do not depend on the browser or HTML.

The Progress Of Async

If JavaScript is essentially an asynchronous language, why has it taken so long for it to develop the sophisticated features it has today?

The story of async in JavaScript provides the structure of this book. We start in Chapter 2 where JavaScript started with events. Events are generated mainly by the UI and what happens is determined by the event handlers assigned to the event. This is where asynchronous programming starts and it is important to fully understand what is going on, so Chapter 3 is also about working with events and, in particular, implementing your own true async events.

Events are where asynchronous programming starts, but it quickly becomes apparent that you need additional ways of dealing with long running tasks. The most basic solution is the callback and this is where async programming starts to become difficult. Chapter 3 explains the relationship between events and callbacks and what exactly it is that makes the callback more difficult to manage.

Most callbacks are used with system provided async functions, but there are times when it would be advantageous to implement your own. Chapter 4 explains how to create custom asynchronous programs using callbacks and ways of implementing freeing the UI thread.

JavaScript used to be a single-threaded language, but with the introduction of the Web Worker you can write multi-threaded programs. Chapter 5 explains the basics of worker threads and how to communicate between threads. It also tackles the problem of keeping a worker thread responsive. It turns out that, just because you have multiple threads, it doesn't mean you can forget all you have learned about async programming.

Even though JavaScript has ways of working with callbacks and threads, it still lacks a good way of organizing async programs. This was addressed with the introduction of the Promise object in ES6. Promises were available before ES6, but only if you used a library like jQuery. Promises in ES6 are covered in Chapters 6 and 7 where we first look at how to use functions that return Promises, i.e. how to consume them, and then we look at how to create functions that make use of Promises, i.e. how to produce them.

Promises are the pinnacle of async programming in JavaScript and Chapter 8 returns to the ways that the dispatch queue can be used, bringing together all we've already covered about event handling and covering some of its more subtle aspects.

Promises are a great idea, but they can be subtle and sometime tricky to use properly. However, combined with the new async and await instructions they suddenly become very easy to use. Chapter 9 explains how async and await work and how they interact with Promises. It is true to say that async and await make async programming as easy as it can be, but you only really get the best out of them if you fully understand how they make use of Promises. The way that async and await work with Promises is nothing short of amazing.

Chapter 10 makes use of async and await to work with some of the latest JavaScript APIs that are based on the Promise object. The Service Worker is possibly the biggest change in the way JavaScript can be used to create programs that are just as happy being offline as online.

The Future Of Asynchronous Programming

It remains to be seen if async and await are the last words in making asynchronous programming easy, but at the moment they certainly seem to be. There are some more features making their way into JavaScript, notably async iterators and generators, but compared to the Promise revolution these are small details.

In many ways events are where asynchronous programming begins and in this context it is a fairly natural approach.

We first need to delve into events to find out how their basic behavior affects the way JavaScript works and how best to think about it. Asynchronous code is a big topic, but events are where it all starts.

JavaScript is essentially an asynchronous language because of events and until recently it was just a single-threaded language. This too is something that affects the way JavaScript works and the way that we use it.

So what exactly is this "asynchronous" behavior all about?

The Workings of Async- the Dispatch Queue

JavaScript can be considered to be a single-threaded language.

A thread in this case means thread of execution. A typical machine will have many threads of execution all managed by the operating system. This is how a machine can seem to be doing more than one thing at a time. If the machine actually has multiple cores then it can really be doing more than one thing at a time because each core can run a thread of execution at the same time. Making use of multiple threads in a reliable and bug free way is difficult. So difficult that in many cases it is a good idea to confine programs to just one thread.

A JavaScript program running in a single web page has just one thread of execution – the User Interface or UI thread.

The reason it is generally called the UI thread is that its sole purpose in life is to look after the User Interface. The UI thread simply responds to events generated by the UI.

To mangle an old aviation saying – *a JavaScript program is essentially a collection of event handlers flying in close formation*.

An event is generally something that happens as a result of what the user does. For example, when the user clicks a button, a click event is generated.

What happens is that the dispatcher maintains a queue of requests generated by UI events. Any event that occurs adds a record to the end of the queue with details of what code should be run as a response to the event. The UI

15

thread takes a request from the front of the queue and runs the code associated with the event. When the event code completes the UI thread returns to the queue and deals with another request.

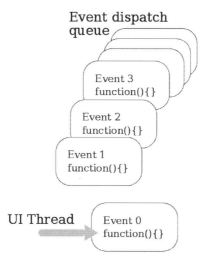

Notice that once the UI thread starts to execute an event handler, it runs to completion of that handler before it moves on to deal with another event from the head of the queue.

This continues until the queue is empty and all of the events have been dealt with. The UI thread then just waits for an event to occur.

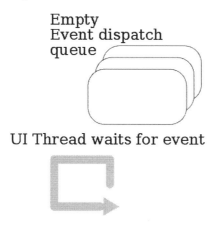

You can see that this means that the user generates events and your program responds to them as quickly as possible and in the order in which they occur, but not necessarily at once.

If you have understood this simple dispatcher mechanism you should be able to understand a great deal of otherwise strange behavior. For example, if you write an event handler that takes a long time to complete then the user interface will appear to freeze because the UI thread cannot process any more events.

In fact for a responsive UI what you really need is for the UI thread to be idle most of the time just waiting for an event to occur. Whenever you are actually making use of the UI thread within an event handler then the user interface is frozen.

The ideal JavaScript program does nothing but wait for a UI event.

The big problem is that as JavaScript is single-threaded and the only thread you have to do any work is the UI thread, you have to find ways of using it that don't make the user interface freeze up.

If you already know that modern JavaScript has the ability to run more than just the UI thread in the form of Web Workers, it is worth pointing out that a Web Worker has its own event queue and works in the same way as the UI thread. In short, Web Workers don't solve the problems of the single-threaded UI in any simple way.

It is also tempting to think that the solution to the problem is to allow multiple threads to work with the UI so that it doesn't freeze if there is a lot of work to do. The problem is that writing reliable multi-threaded programs is difficult. This is the reason that most UIs are single-threaded. There have been attempts in the past to create a UI framework that allows multiple threads to work with it, but it has always proved difficult.

As a result JavaScript and HTML, in line with most UI frameworks, limit access to the UI to a single thread.

That is, you cannot have one thread respond to one button click and another thread responding to another click. In the JavaScript UI things happen one at a time – even if you make use of multiple threads as supplied by Web Workers.

In JavaScript the UI is single-threaded.

Events

The key idea from the previous section is that the natural state of the UI thread is doing nothing. It really should only burst into life to do something in response to an event and get back to waiting for the next event as soon as possible. This raises the question of what exactly an event is?

The simple answer is that mostly event generation has nothing much to do with JavaScript, it is part of the definition of the DOM – the Document Object Model which is the code representation of the UI generated by the HTML.

The DOM isn't part of JavaScript and it is only available when JavaScript is running in a browser. Other environments provide events in slightly different ways, but mostly they look like the events that the DOM generates. The DOM may not be part of JavaScript, but everyone regards it as the standard way to do things. For example, when the user clicks on a button say the button click event is added to the dispatcher's queue. The details of the event are also stored in the queue as an event object. The event object has a range of properties which can be used by the event handler to find out which UI element generated the event and other details. What is stored in the event object depends on the event that occurred and to some extent on the particular browser being used.

When the UI thread is free it takes the event at the head of the queue and calls the event handler, passing it the event object. The event handler responds to the event by doing something appropriate and perhaps using the information about the event stored in the event object.

Notice that when an event handler is running nothing else can happen. The event handler will run until it yields the UI thread by coming to an end, often by performing a return. Events that happen while an event handler is running are added to the dispatcher's queue and they have to wait their turn for the UI thread to run them.

JavaScript programming can be seen as mostly creating event handlers and registering them with objects that can generate events. You could say that the only purpose of a JavaScript function object is to respond to the user, but this might be going a bit too far. Events, however, have to be seen as driving most applications with code being run in response to the events generated by the DOM.

Registering Event Handlers

How do you register a function to an event?

This used to be a problem because different browsers implemented event handling in different ways, but today there is just one standard way of doing the job.

If you need to support older browsers then use jQuery which provides a browser-independent way of working with events.

In HTML you can set an event handler on an element using the well known "on" properties, such as:

```
<button onclick="myEventHandler" ...
```

You can also add an event handler by setting the property in code:

```
document.getElementById("myButton").onclick=function(e){...}
```

Not all events have on properties and therefore cannot be set in this way. Also you can only set a single event handler. Assigning another function to the "on" property simply overwrites the previous value.

In code the modern way of doing the same job is to use the addEventListener method to register the event handler to the target. The target keeps a list of event listeners and so isn't restricted to just one.

For example:

```
button1.addEventListener("click",myEventHandler);
```

will result in myEventHandler being called when the user clicks the button. Notice that while the HTML needs a string which provides the event handlers name, the addEventListener uses the reference to the function object. The first parameter specifies the event as a string.

A good source of information on what event names you can use can be found in MDN web docs – https://developer.mozilla.org/en-US/docs/Web/Events.

You can also remove an event handler using:

```
removeEventListener(type,function,useCapture)
```

Notice that the type and function have to match exactly the event handler added.

Removing event handlers is something of a problem. There is currently no way to get a list of events that are registered to an object. This is fixed in DOM 3, but at the moment this isn't implemented in any of the modern browsers. If you want to remove event handlers you have to keep track of them yourself and this means not using anonymous functions which are currently difficult, if not impossible, to remove.

Multiple Event Handlers

One small point that is often overlooked is that an event source can have more than one event handler registered with it using addEventListener.

It is customary to call event handlers added using addEventListener "event listeners", but the term "event handler" can be used for anything that responds to an event.

For example:

```
button1.addEventListener("click",myEventHandler1);
button1.addEventListener("click",myEventHandler2);

function myEventHandler1(e){
 alert("event1");
}

function myEventHandler2(e){
 alert("event2");
}
```

When the button is clicked you will see two alerts, one per event handler.

Notice that there is no guarantee as to the order in which event handlers are called.

Why would you register multiple event handlers?

In many cases it doesn't make sense to use more than one event handler.

The reason is that an event occurs and it is clear and simple what should happen. The user clicks a Save button and the click event should result in a click event handler being called that saves the data. One event – one handler.

However, there are times when this isn't the case because an event is associated with multiple unrelated logical actions. You might have a Save button that saves the data and incidentally shows the user an ad. In this case it makes sense to keep the functions separate. Notice that there is no way to make sure that the ad is shown before the save or vice versa.

If you demand determinate actions then you need to use jQuery's implementation of JavaScript events – see *Just jQuery: Events, Async & Ajax* (ISBN: 978-1871962529). Alternatively you could just put the calls to the two separate functions in a single event handler.

Bubbling and Capture

We also have to consider the way events work in the DOM. In particular, the way events "bubble".

In an HTML page different UI elements are nested inside one another. For example:

```
<div id="div1">
    Some Text
  <button id="button1">Click me</button>
</div>
```

defines a button contained inside a div. If we now define an event handler for each:

```
div1.addEventListener("click",myEventHandler1);
button1.addEventListener("click",myEventHandler2);
function myEventHandler1(e){ alert("div"); }
function myEventHandler2(e){ alert("button"); }
```

we can discover what happens when an event occurs on the inner UI element, i.e. the button. With event bubbling, the innermost item handles the event first and then passes it up in turn to the outer items. So, if you click on the button you will see the button alert and then the div alert.

Why do we want events to bubble?

The reason is that there might be an action which has to be performed by the containing UI element when a child element is used. For example, the div event handler might reset all of the child buttons it contains. It might also be the case that you don't want to implement event handlers for all of the inner elements. In this case you could allow the event to bubble up to the outermost UI element and handle it there. Notice that the event object passed to the handler can be used to find out what UI element the event actually occurred on.

For example, if you define three buttons within a div you can handle a click on any button with an event handler registered to the div simply because the button click events bubble up:

```
<div id="div1">
 <button id="button1">Click me</button>
 <button id="button2">Click me</button>
 <button id="button3">Click me</button>
</div>
<script>
  div1.addEventListener("click",myEventHandler1);
  function myEventHandler1(e){
   alert(e.target.id);
  }
</script>
```

When you click on any button the alert box correctly shows the id of the button. By default all events bubble up the UI hierarchy.

The other way to allow events to propagate is called capture and this can be thought of as bubbling down, and is sometimes called trickling down. In this case, when an event occurs on an inner UI element it is the topmost enclosing UI element that gets to handle the event first.

To select capture you have to specify a third parameter – useCapture – when registering the event handler.

Changing the previous example of a button inside a div to use capture gives:

```
<div id="div1">
    Some Text
    <button id="button1">Click me</button></div>
<script>
 div1.addEventListener("click",myEventHandler1,true);
 button1.addEventListener("click",myEventHandler2);

 function myEventHandler1(e){ alert("div"); }
 function myEventHandler2(e){ alert("button"); }
</script>
```

Notice that the div event handler is now registered with useCapture set to true. This means that all click events that occur on UI elements that are contained by it are handled by it and then passed down through child elements back to the element that the event occurred on. Now if you click on the button you will see the div message first and the button message second.

In most cases it is much simpler to use bubbling because older browsers don't support capture.

Controlling Events

As well as providing information about the event, the Event object also has some methods that let you control and inquire about the state of the event.

Many events have a default action. For example, clicking on a link loads that page into the browser. You can stop default actions using:

```
event.preventDefault();
```

You can discover if some other event handler had prevented the default action using:

```
event.isDefaultPrevented();
```

You can also stop bubbling and/or capture using either:

```
event.stopPropagation();
```

or:

```
event.stopImmediatePropagation();
```

which stops any other event handler being called even if it is attached to the same object.

You can test to see if bubbling has been stopped using:

```
event.isPropagationStopped();
```

Compatibility

Event handling in older browsers is a mess. You can spend a lot of time trying to write event handling code that works as widely as possible, but it is better to simply give in and use jQuery which smooths out the differences.

For example in Internet Explorer 8 and earlier you have to use attachEvent in place of addEventListener. There are also big variations in what information is passed to the event handler via the event object. Even in modern browsers there is a great deal of variation in the implementation of the options that are allowed. For example, at the time of writing Edge doesn't fully support the options parameter.

There is also the problem of what events are available. The most common events click, focus and so on are supported in a uniform fashion, but there are many events relating to specific hardware, mobile and touch hardware in particular, that are not implemented uniformly across all browsers. For example, only the very latest browsers support WheelEvent - which replaces the nonstandard MouseWheelEvent. Even worse is the TouchEvent which isn't supported on Opera, IE or Safari. Most touch-based events are not supported by IE, Opera or Safari.

If you are going to use any touch or other hardware-based events other then the very common mouse related events then you need to check which browsers support them.

Custom Events

Normally events are fired by the browser or the more general environment that JavaScript is running in. Sometimes it is useful to be able to originate an event, either an existing event type or a completely new event type under program control.

The simplest way to fire an event is to use the HTMLElement event methods click, focus, blur, submit and reset. All HTMLElements support click, but the rest vary in what they support - obviously only a form element supports submit or reset for example.

Firing other events is more problematic as browsers vary in what they support.

The modern way to fire an event is to construct an event object and then pass it as a parameter in dispatchEvent:

```
var event = new MouseEvent('click', {
                              'bubbles': true,
                              'cancelable': true
                            });
button1.dispatchEvent(event);
```

If there isn't a constructor for the particular event you want to use, simply use the general Event constructor.

```
var event = new Event('click');
button1.dispatchEvent(event);
```

The difference is that the most specific constructor has additional methods and properties that make setting up that particular type of event easier.

The older createEvent method is deprecated, but still widely supported.

As well as firing predefined events you can also create and fire custom events. All you have to do is use an event name that is suitable and consistent. For example:

```
var event = new Event('myEvent', {
                            'bubbles': true,
                            'cancelable': true
                          });
button1.addEventListener("myEvent",
                          function(e){
                            console.log("MyEvent");
                          });
button1.dispatchEvent(event);
```

Notice that myEvent isn't a system event, but one we just made up.

If you want to include some custom data then you need to use the CustomEvent constructor and pass the data in the detail property:

```
var event = new CustomEvent('myEvent', {detail: "myData"});
```

However, you don't have to use a CustomEvent object to implement a custom event – only if you want to pass custom data to a custom event.

Asynchronous Custom Events

There is a small problem with custom events – they aren't really events.

Consider the following code:

```
var event = new Event('myEvent', {
                              'bubbles': true,
                              'cancelable': true
                            });
button1.addEventListener("myEvent",
                            function(e){
                               console.log("MyEvent");
                            });

console.log("Before Event");
button1.dispatchEvent(event);
console.log("After Event")
```

what would you expect to see displayed in the console?

What you actually see is:

```
Before Event
MyEvent
After Event
```

You might at first glance think that this is what you would expect, but wait, the MyEvent message is displayed as the result of an event and the Before and After messages are displayed within the same code which isn't part of the event handler.

What should happen when the event is dispatched is that the event should be added to the dispatch queue and the current code should run to completion. Only then is the UI thread handed back to the dispatcher which then runs whatever event is top of the dispatch queue. In other word what you should see is:

```
Before Event
After Event
MyEvent
```

and perhaps some other events might be processed before MyEvent gets its turn.

The dispatchEvent method is more like a function call than an event invocation. The point is that function calls are synchronous in the sense that the calling function waits for the called function to complete. An event, however, is supposed to be asynchronous and the function that triggers the event should run to completion before the event is handled.

Normally JavaScript ensures that no events will be handled until your code completes, but if you use dispatchEvent this is no longer true.

You can create true asynchronous events if you want to.

All you have to do is find a way to add a function call to the dispatch queue. This is a topic that will crop up a number of times as we look at different aspects of asynchronous programming, but it is discussed in depth in Chapter 9.

The simplest way to add something to the dispatch queue is to use the setTimeout function. This will place a message in the event queue that calls a function after a set time. That is:

```
setTimeout(function,delay);
```

will call the function after the specified delay in milliseconds.

A better way to think of this is that the function will be added to the dispatch queue after the delay. Notice that this means that the function will not be executed until the delay is up, but it won't necessarily be executed immediately after that. It could sit in the dispatch queue for an indefinite period until the UI thread had time to process it. Hence the delay specified is the minimum time before the function is executed.

If you don't specify a delay then the default is zero.

You may already be familiar with this function as a way of calling functions after a delay, but it can also be used to create a custom asynchronous event.

All you have to do is call setTimeout with a delay of zero and use it to dispatch the event:

```
console.log("Before Event");
setTimeout(function(){
          button1.dispatchEvent(event);
        },0);
console.log("After Event")
```

This effectively puts the dispatching function on the event queue and then returns immediately. Of course, the function will not be processed by the event queue until the UI thread is released and so now what you see is:

```
Before Event
After Event
MyEvent
```

which is the asynchronous behavior of a true event.

In practice you can wrap the setTimeout in a suitable function and hide a little of what is going on:

```
function fireEvent(elem, ev) {
 var event = new Event(ev, {
                            'bubbles': true,
                            'cancelable': true
                          });

 setTimeout(function(){
            elem.dispatchEvent(event);
            },0);
}
```

With this function defined we can simply write:

```
console.log("Before Event");
fireEvent(button1, "myEvent");
console.log("After Event");
```

The difference between synchronous and asynchronous events is important – make sure you are using the correct implementation..

A Fast Asynchronous Custom Event

SetTimeout is a very convenient way of getting a function to behave asynchronously. It is widely supported and you can regard it as a "just works" solution. However, it has a problem in that it can be slow. You might specify a delay of zero milliseconds, but it is more likely to be tens of milliseconds before the function runs. This is not only because of the UI thread being in use it is also because browsers apply a minimum delay time, typically 4ms. That is even if the UI thread is not doing anything else it can still take 4ms to fire an event. This translates to a maximum rate of about 200 events per second. Using the method described below you can generate closer to 20,000 events per second.

If you demand the fastest custom event handling then you need to make use of the window.postMessage method. Its downside is that it is only supported in modern browsers with only partial support in IE 11.

In general postMessage can be used to fire a message event in another window, but it is faster to send the message to the same window:

```
window.postMessage("fireEvent", "*");
```

This places a message event into the event queue with the message payload "fireEvent", As soon as the UI thread is free to process events a message event occurs on the current window.

There is no minimum delay in using postMessage.

A version of the fireEvent utility function using postMessage is easy to create:

```
function fireEvent(elem, ev) {
 var event = new Event(ev);
 var fire = function (e) {
             elem.dispatchEvent(event);
             window.removeEventListener("message", fire, false);
          };
 window.addEventListener("message", fire, false);
 window.postMessage("fireEvent", "*");
}
```

The fireEvent function first creates the custom event object and then adds the function fire to respond to the message event. Finally it fires the message event using postMessage. When the UI thread is freed the message event occurs and triggers fire which in turn runs the custom event and removes fire as a message event handler so that it will not be accidentally triggered again.

You can, of course, improve on this function and you might want to leave an event handler attached to the window message event ready to handle custom events.

What Is the Main Program For?

A JavaScript program is a collection of event handlers. This raises the question of what code that is outside of an event handler is for?

JavaScript is different from many other languages in that it doesn't have a "main" function i.e. a function which is called to get the program started. Instead you simply write instructions at a "global" level outside of any function and they are executed sequentially from top-to-bottom and left-to-right.

Notice that, as JavaScript is single-threaded, no events can be serviced while the global code is being executed.

The only purpose of global code in an event-driven architecture is to perform initialization. You write global code to set up event handlers and do any other initialization that is essential. As is the case with all JavaScript code, it is important that the global code is short and does not keep the UI thread occupied for too long. It is a beginners mistake to put a delay or a pause in the global code, but giving the UI thread too much to do when your program first starts is a mistake we all make.

The global code is run at the point in the page load where it occurs. If you want to run your JavaScript at a precise point in the page load it is better to convert global code into just another event handler.

You can use the DOMContentLoaded event to start your code running when the DOM is ready to be worked with, but the page might not have finished loading because of images and style sheets etc still being downloaded:

```
document.addEventListener('DOMContentLoaded', function() {…});
```

This works on most browsers, but not IE8 and earlier. If you need the entire page to be loaded then use the load event:

```
window.addEventListener("load", function() {…});
```

The most important thing to remember is that it is good practice to have as little global code as possible.

Why Is Event-Driven Code Asynchronous?

We gain an understanding of what asynchronous code is by writing it, but why exactly do we call event-driven architecture "asynchronous"? The definition in Google's dictionary that is most appropriate is:

> *controlling the timing of operations by the use of pulses sent when the previous operation is completed rather than at regular intervals.*

Events don't occur in any particular order and this means that event handlers don't run in any particular order. In synchronous code every instruction has a specific place in the program and the order of execution is fixed by the program and the data. Another way to say this is that the order of execution is fixed and deterministic, whereas asynchronous code looks almost random as it responds to the outside world.

Things not happening in a fixed order is one of the main signatures of asynchronous code.

Summary

- The JavaScript UI is single-threaded.

- The dispatcher uses the UI thread to handle events. When an event happens it is added to the dispatch queue and the dispatcher allows each event to execute on the UI thread in turn.

- Once an event handler has the UI thread it keeps it until it has finished.

- This means that while any JavaScript code is running no other event can be handled and the UI is unresponsive.

- If an event handler runs for a long time then the user will notice that the UI has frozen.

- The ideal JavaScript program does nothing but leave the UI thread idle waiting to service an event.

- You can add event handlers to an object using its addEventListener method.

- An object can have multiple event handlers in its event listener list.

- Bubbling and capture make event handling most sophisticated and implementation simpler.

- You can trigger an event, existing or custom, using the object's dispatchEvent method with a suitable Event object.

- The dispatchEvent method behaves more like a function call than a true event. That is, it creates a synchronous event.

- If you need a true asynchronous event then you need to use the setTimeout or postMessage method to add a function which triggers the event to the dispatch queue.

- A JavaScript program is a collection of event handlers, the only purpose the main or global code serves is to initialize things.

Chapter 3

The Callback

Events are the first place you are likely to meet asynchronous functions, but once you have events and an event dispatching system you can't stop there. Any long running function has to be implemented as an asynchronous non-blocking function if the UI is to remain responsive. This causes all sorts of difficulties that go beyond events and event handling.

Most of the rest of this book is about implementing and managing asynchronous functions and we will tackle the same fundamental problem from a number of points of view. In this chapter we take the most basic viewpoint and look at the idea of the callback.

Events versus Asynchronous Functions

There really is no need to go any further than events when you consider asynchronous functions. However, for historical reasons we need to look at asynchronous functions that arise in a non-event form in a slightly different way.

The problem arises because of the need to manage the UI thread. If you have an event handler that needs to do some extended work it has to give up the UI thread now and again to keep the UI functioning. This simple fact colors all of JavaScript programming. It is what makes JavaScript programming difficult. The same is true of any language that has to cope with a single-threaded UI.

The problem is made worse by the fact that long running functions are often long running because they ask the system to do something. In this case another thread or an interrupt is involved to make the process run in the background. For example when you ask for a file to be loaded the UI thread doesn't actually do the file load. Instead the task is handed off to the operating system. The UI thread could just wait for the file to be ready, but this would block the UI and so generally this isn't what happens.

This gives rise to the idea that the behavior of a function call can be be blocking or non-blocking.

What does this mean?

All functions return, eventually, and a blocking function returns when its work is done. A non-blocking function, on the other hand, returns when its work is set in motion.

That is, a blocking function returns with its result, but a non-blocking function simply returns with an expectation that its work will be done sometime in the future and its result will be available.

How can you get the result of a non-blocking function?

This is why general asynchronous programming is difficult. The use of a non-blocking function distorts the flow of control. Normally with a blocking function, when the function returns you can just get on with the algorithm. If the function was downloading a file you can now get on with processing that file. If the function was non-blocking, then you can't get on because the result, the file, isn't available. In this case you have no choice but to give the UI thread back and wait for the result to be available.

The standard solution is to provide a callback function to the non-blocking function.

A callback is a function that the non-blocking process calls when it has really finished its task.

As functions are first class objects in JavaScript, using callbacks is relatively easy – you don't have to invent extra ideas such as delegates (C#), anonymous classes (Java) and lambdas (almost all languages) - to pass a function as a parameter. In fact, you almost certainly have been using callbacks for a long time, perhaps without realizing their connection to events.

A callback is like an event handler which fires when the non-blocking function completes its task.

In fact there is little reason to invent the callback. It would be simpler to define task completion events and register event handlers for the event.

For example, suppose we have getFile function which returns a file after using AJAX to download it. The callback version of the function would be used something like:

```
getFile(url,callback)
```

and would return at once and call the callback function sometime later when the file had been downloaded.

This can be converted into an event by introducing an object that an event can be attached to:

```
var ajax={};
ajax.getfile=function(url){ getFile(url,
                  function(){
                   var event = new Event("FileLoaded",
                                         {
                                          'bubbles': true,
                                          'cancelable': true
                                         });
                   ajax.dispatchEvent(event);
                  });
          };
```

When the getfile function is used it still returns without blocking, but now it raises the FileLoaded event when the file is ready to be processed. To use the new function you would attach an event handler rather than specify a callback:

```
ajax.addEventListener("FileLoaded",eventHandler);
getfile(url);
```

Event handler or callback – its a choice.

The Problem With Asynchronous

Callbacks may be like event handlers, but the way that they occur in code makes them a very different proposition. You might be able to implement callbacks as events, but they have some important differences.

Event handlers are in the main easy to write and cause few problems, but callbacks have some serious problems. The reason for this difference is that event handlers are set up by code that has no interest in their results.

Event handlers generally don't do anything that the code that sets them up cares about.

When you set a button's click handler, the code that sets it generally doesn't want to interact with the click handler later in time when a click occurs. It's a set and forget operation. In other words, event handlers are usually fairly closed pieces of code that don't depend on anything other than the event that just occurred and the global state of the program.

Callbacks, on the other hand, generally do something that the code that sets them up cares about.

Generally you want to download a file and process the data it contains. In an ideal world the download would complete and then the code would continue on its way to process the file. When you have to use a callback this isn't the way it happens – the process is initiated and the code that started it comes to an end; only later does the callback activate and the process is completed elsewhere.

There is a real sense in which a callback is a continuation of the program that called the non-blocking function, whereas an event handler isn't a continuation of any particular part of the program.

This is more difficult.

You will hear lots of explanations of the problem of asynchronous code along the lines of "callback hell", and the "callback pyramid of doom". These are problems, but they arise from taking particular approaches to asynchronous programming.

The first problem is that raw asynchronous programming distorts the intended flow of control.

In a synchronous program you might write:

```
loadA();
loadB();
loadC();
```

and you can expect A to load before B which loads before C.

As soon as you convert these to async operations you can't be sure what order things are done in unless you adopt the callback cascade:

```
loadA(loadB(loadC()));
```

where each function accepts a callback as its parameter. That is, loadA calls loadB as soon as its file is downloaded and then loadB calls loadC when its file is downloaded. Each callback determines what is to happen next.

The callback approach to async turns sequential default flow of control into nested function calls.

But keep in mind that the callback approach is just one of many. Because it is so widely used, there is a tendency to think that a callback is the only way to deal with asynchronous code. As we have already seen, we can avoid callbacks by implementing events that are fired when the non-blocking function has finished its task and the program can continue from where it left off.

Before you conclude that using events instead of callbacks is a better way of doing things, notice that events convert the sequential flow of control into nested events.

For example, assuming that we have objects loadA, loadB and loadC that fire the loaded event when their get method completes:

```
loadA.addEventListener("loaded",function(fileA){loadB.get()}
loadB.addEventListener("loaded",function(fileB){loadC.get()}
loadC.addEventListener("loaded",function(fileC){...}
loadA.get()
```

Which isn't a lot better than the nested callbacks. In this case the event handlers are set up first and then the first file load is started. This triggers the loaded event which in turn starts the second file loading. In the real world each event handler would also process the file that had been loaded. This is just as much a distortion of the sequential flow of control that we are trying to implement as a callback.

Notice that the sequential flow of control is the simplest and things become much more difficult if you try to implement conditionals or loops which involve non-blocking functions.

Put simply the need to yield the UI thread before the task is complete is a major disruption to the flow of control.

Asynchronous Flow of Control and Closure

The effect that asynchronous code has on the structure of your program is easy to understand in terms of what code goes before and what code goes after the task in question. If we first consider the structure of the program using a blocking version of LoadA:

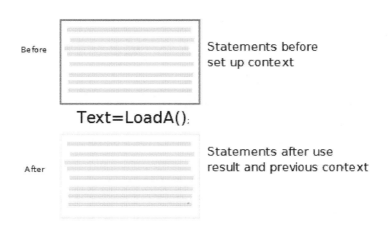

The statements that are before the task i.e the call to LoadA provide the context for the call. Variables which are set in this "before" code may contain values that are important for what to do with the result of the task and in the code to follow it. The code that follows it makes use of the result of the operation and the context established by the earlier code. This is simply the expression of the fact that code generally tends to use results from code that has executed earlier.

When you convert the task to a non-blocking function and use a callback the code that follows the call to the asynchronous function doesn't follow in this natural way – it becomes another function.

That is, the "after" code becomes the callback:

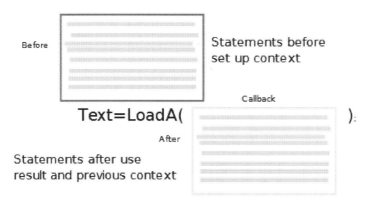

You can now see that the flow of control has been distorted – what was one function is now two. Don't worry too much about it at the moment, but this isn't a complete picture of what can happen because if the Callback contains an asynchronous call you repeat the procedure of moving the "after" code into a callback – distorting the flow of control again. It is even a good question what the Text variable is set to. After all it can't be the result of the task as this hasn't completed when it returns. For the moment just assume that Text is set to some value that the function provides.

Not only is the flow of control distorted, in a simple programming environment the context is lost. As the "after" code is now a separate function it no longer has access to the variables contained in the "before" code. In short, the callback can't perform an instruction like i=i+1 because i isn't only out of scope, it doesn't even exist any more.

Except, of course, in JavaScript the call context is preserved.

JavaScript supports closure and this means that the variables that were in scope when a function was created remain in scope for it even if from the point of view of other parts of the program they have long been destroyed. That means the callback does have access to the variable i and can perform i=i+1 because closure provides all of the variables that were defined when it was.

There are many complex and esoteric explanations of what closure is and why you might want it, but it is this automatic provision of context to a callback function that seems the most convincing. There are lots of other uses of closure, but it is this one that you would invent closure for – to join up the two parts of the program that were together before you used a non-blocking function and a callback.

Closures ensure that callbacks have their context.

Of course things can be more complicated. It could be that the asynchronous function call is itself nested within a control structure that spans the before and after block of code.

For example, if a callback is in a for loop then the loop executes and completes, possibly before any of the callbacks are activated. Similarly, an if statement cannot test the result of a callback because this isn't available at the time the code is executed.

Closures solve many of the problems of callbacks, but not all.

Finally it is worth making the point again that the existence of and need to access their call context is one of the big differences between a callback and an event handler. When an event handler is fired it doesn't have the concept of a calling function involved in its activation and the only context it makes use of is that passed by the Event object and the global state of the program.

Asynchronous Errors

It is clear that using callbacks makes a mess of the flow of control of a program and it is difficult to ensure that everything happens in the correct order. However, often the order in which callbacks occur isn't important.

For example, if you are loading a set of files it usually doesn't matter what order they are loaded in as long they do load and are processed.

A more common problem, and one that is often ignored, is what should happen when an error occurs. It has to be admitted that this is often a problem in synchronous code as well.

The big difference in asynchronous code is that the error problem can occur at any time after the callbacks have been set and in any order.

In a synchronous blocking program you might write:

```
try{
 load A
 load B
 load C
}
catch(e){
 deal with a problem
}
```

If you change the load functions to asynchronous functions then the catch doesn't catch any of the errors that the loads might produce, and certainly not any that the callbacks might create. The reason is simply that the catch clause is executed before any of this code actually runs and it is well in the past when any errors might actually occur.

Handling errors is a big problem for asynchronous programs because it is difficult to know the state of the system when the error occurs. If file B fails to download what to do might depend on whether file A or C downloaded or not. The simplest way of dealing with errors is to provide an alternative callback that is used if the asynchronous function fails.

For example:

```
load(A,success,error)
```

where success is called if the load works and error is called otherwise.

This is easy to propose as a solution and much more difficult to make work in practice. The problem is that the error function generally has no way to determine the overall state of the transactions that might still be in progress and generally no easy way to stop them. For example there is no AJAX abort operation to stop a file download.

Async makes error handling more difficult, but it was difficult to start with.

Controlling Callback Flow of Control – Sequential

As we have already seen you can implement a sequential flow of control using callbacks. All you have to do is place a call to the next operation in each callback.

This works, but there are a number of techniques that you can use to simplify or automate the sequential calling of non-blocking functions with callbacks.

All of these make use of a controlling object or sequencer. For example, jQuery has its function queue which can be used to execute one non-blocking task after another. The problem with all of these schemes is that they are either limited or become increasingly complex to cope with more general situations. However, this said, for simple situations they are worth considering as alternatives to more sophisticated solutions such as Promises.

The key idea is that you make use of a controller object which provides methods to manage the execution of the non-blocking functions. In general the object has an add method to allow you to add a function to the queue, and a method to start execution of the queue.

For example we can define a simple controller object with an add method:

```
var controller = {};
controller.queue= [];
controller.add = function (func) {
                controller.queue.push(func);
                };
```

In this case the controller object is defined as a singleton, but you can create a constructor if you need multiple instances. You can also use the standard techniques to make the queue private.

The controller has an array that is used as a FIFO queue. The add method simply adds the non-blocking function to the queue.

If we assume that each non-blocking function accepts a single parameter which is the callback we can start things moving using:

```
controller.run =
            function () {
             controller.queue.shift()(controller.run);
            };
```

This takes the function on the head of the queue and runs it passing the run method as the callback. This means that when each non-blocking function ends it starts the next function going, as its callback is the run method which always runs the next function in the queue.

For example if the non-blocking functions are:

```
function longRunA(callback) {
 console.log("A");
 setTimeout(callback, 2000);
}
function longRunB(callback) {
 console.log("B");
 setTimeout(callback, 1000);
}
```

Then just calling the functions results in A being printed followed more or less immediately by B.

However, using:
```
controller.add(longRunA);
controller.add(longRunB);
controller.run();
```
Results in A being printed followed by B after 2 seconds. That is, longRunB only starts after longRunA ends.

This is simpler and arguably better than nested callbacks, but it has problems of its own. In particular, the functions that are in the queue have to have a known set of parameters so that they can be called correctly.

For example in this case each non-blocking function only accepts a callback. Also in this case the callback doesn't do any processing. All of these limitations can be overcome, but only at the cost of increased complexity.

You can also arrange for a controller object to call non-blocking functions a number of times or conditionally, so allowing you to implement the standard types of flow of control asynchronously. The problem is the same as for the simple sequential flow, however.

The controller object has to be crafted to suit your particular needs or it has to be complex to achieve a generality.

The common idea is that the callback passed to the non-blocking function is a method of the controller object which is used to perform the next action.

For example, to extend the controller so that it can repeat a non-blocking function a set number of times:
```
controller.count=0;
controller.current=0;
controller.repeat=function(n){
            controller.count=n;
            controller.current=controller.queue.shift();
            controller.next();
          };
controller.next=function(){
          if(controller.count===0)return;
          controller.count-=1;
          controller.current(controller.next);
          };
```
The repeat method gets the iteration started and the next method moves it on one and terminates it when the count has been exhausted. For example:
```
controller.add(longRunA);
controller.repeat(3);
```
repeats longRunA three times.

You can see how you could turn repeat into say a timeout with a retry function or test the return value for success or failure etc.

The controller method is particularly appropriate if what you are trying to do fits the finite state model. Then you can provide the controller with a state variable, call non-blocking functions, and change the state depending on the results as they happen.

However, this said, in most cases what you want to do is not regular enough for this approach and Promises or async/await are a better option.

Summary

- To keep the UI active long running functions are non-blocking and return the UI thread before they have finished their work.

- Non-blocking functions make use of callbacks or events to process the results of their work.

- Callbacks are like event handlers, but they generally make use of the context they were called from.

- Closure allows a callback to access its call context.

- Asynchronous code distorts the flow of control – sequential execution becomes nested callbacks.

- Asynchronous code makes error handling more difficult than it already is.

- One way to implement the traditional flow of control using asynchronous functions is to implement a controller object which has methods that are used as callbacks.

- Controllers work well if the situation can be implemented as a state machine.

Chapter 4
Custom Async

If you want to write JavaScript apps that are responsive, you have little choice but to master the art of creating your own non-blocking asynchronous functions. In this chapter we look at ways of working with the event queue to keep the UI working.

To keep the UI responsive you have to let the UI thread do its job – which is to service the UI. There are only two ways to do this:

- you can opt to do your computation on the UI thread and arrange to release it frequently enough for it not to be missed

or

- you can use a separate thread of execution.

In many ways using a separate thread is the best possible solution and it is the subject of the next chapter. However, using worker threads has its drawbacks. The biggest is that it isn't supported on all browsers and when it is some features vary. It can be difficult to write a multi-threaded program that works on all modern browsers.

There is also the problem of passing data between the threads and updating the UI in particular. For many simple cases managing the UI thread to do the work is an attractive option and it is certainly worth knowing what techniques are available to you to do so.

Custom Non-Blocking Functions

JavaScript has a number of non-blocking functions, mostly to do with downloading files, and when you make use of them you have write asynchronous code. However, the story doesn't stop with supplied functions. If you have any difficult task to perform it has to be implemented as a non-blocking custom function.

Key to doing this in a way that will work on almost any browser and version of JavaScript is the setTimeout function that we met in chapter Two. This will place a message in the event queue that calls a function after a set time.

If you need a super efficient custom non-blocking function then you can use postMessage to add to the event queue without a minimum delay and this was also introduced in chapter Two.

But for simplicity let's start with setTimeout and return to postMessage later. We have already used them to implement true custom events, but their use in more general custom non-blocking functions is more important and worth going over again.

All you have to do is call setTimeout with a delay of zero:

```
setTimeout(function(){do something},0);
```

This effectively puts the function on the event queue and then returns immediately. Of course, the function will not be processed by the event queue until the UI thread is released.

A simple example should make this clear:

```
console.log("before");
setTimeout(function () {
        console.log("MyAsyncFunction");
    }, 0);
console.log("after");
```

The sequence of events is that first "before" is sent to the log, then the function is added to the event queue with a timeout of 0, but the function cannot be called until the UI thread is freed. The setTimeout returns at once and "after" is sent to the log and the UI thread is freed, assuming this is the last JavaScript instruction. Only then does the function get to run and send "MyAsyncFunction" to the log.

You can see that the order of execution is not what you might expect, and this is typical asynchronous behavior. Notice also that the event queue is processed in whatever order the events occurred in, and if there is an event waiting to be processed it could be done before your custom function is called.

You can make use of this to break up a long running function so as to keep the UI responsive.

We have to arrange for the function to be "minimally" blocking by managing its use of the UI thread.

If you can't or don't want to use another thread then you have no choice but to divide up the calculation into small chunks. Each chunk should take a short enough time for the user not to notice that the UI isn't being serviced. The function has to restart after the break and it has to continue from where it left off. Notice that this introduces a new consideration into the mix and this is not just a matter of implementing a callback to use an existing non-blocking function, nor is it as simple as implementing a custom async event.

The general idea is very simple, but the details vary according to the algorithm.

A Piece of Pi

As a simple example, suppose you want to compute pi to a few digits using the series:

```
pi=4*(1-1/3+1/5-1/7 ... )
```

This is very easy to implement, we just need to generate the odd integers but to get pi to a reasonable number of digits you have to compute a lot of terms.

The simple-minded synchronous approach is to write something like:

```
button1.click(computePi);

function computePi() {
 var pi = 0;
 var k;
 for (k = 1; k <= 100000; k++) {
  pi += 4 * Math.pow(-1, k + 1) / (2 * k - 1);
  result.innerHTML=pi;
  count.innerHTML=k;
 }
}
```

where the DOM elements are provided by:

```
<div id="result">
0
</div>
<div id="count">
0
</div>
<button id="button1" onclick>Go</button>
```

The intention is to display the progress of the calculation by changing the text displayed in the two divs each time through the for loop. If you try it out what you will find is that the UI freezes for some minutes and nothing is displayed in the web page until the loop finishes and the UI thread is freed to tend to the UI.

Restoring State

This is an example of an unacceptable function that monopolizes the UI thread at the expense of the UI.

To keep the UI responsive, and in this case to see the intermediate results, we have to turn the calculation into an asynchronous function using setTimeout. We do this by breaking the calculation in small chunks – say 1000 iterations each. To do this we need a state object that records the state of the calculation so that it can be resumed:

```
var state = {};
state.k = 0;
state.pi = 0;
```

The function is now going to perform 1000 iterations and then update the text in the divs.

To enable the UI to stay responsive, the function then terminates, but not before setting itself up in the event queue ready to perform another 1000 iterations after the UI has been updated:

```
function computePi() {
 if (state.k >= 100000000) return;
 var i;
 for (i = 0; i < 1000; i++) {
 state.k++;
 state.pi += 4 * Math.pow(-1, state.k + 1)/(2 * state.k - 1);
 }
 result.innerHTML=state.pi;
 count.innerHTML=state.k;
 setTimeout(computePi, 0);
}
```

Notice the final setTimeout which ensures that the function restarts.

If you run this version of the computation you will find that not only does the UI remain responsive, you get to see the intermediate values as the calculation proceeds.

Notice that the computePi function is now almost non-blocking in that it returns after doing 1000 iterations.

Non-Global State

In the previous example the function is able to access the state object because it is a global variable. If you don't want to use a global variable then create the computePi function inside another function and rely on closure to make the state variable accessible e.g:

```
function computePiAsync(){
 var state = {};
 state.k = 0;
 state.pi = 0;
 function computePi() {
  if (state.k >= 100000000) return;
  var i;
  for (i = 0; i < 1000; i++) {
   state.k++;
   state.pi +=4 * Math.pow(-1, state.k + 1) / (2 * state.k - 1);
  }
  result.innerHTML=state.pi;
  count.innerHTML=state.k;
  setTimeout(computePi, 0);
 }
 setTimeout(computePi, 0);
};
```

Using postMessage

We have already discovered in Chapter Two that the problem with using setTimeout is that it is slow. It can take 4 to 5 milliseconds to get the function that computes Pi restarted. The solution in most cases is to use the postMessage method as described in Chapter Two which has a much smaller overhead.

As already explained, the postMessage method of the Window object was introduced to allow JavaScript to pass data between different windows by using events – that is it fires a message event to let the UI thread know that there is a message waiting. However, as it is possible for a window to send itself a message, it can be used as an alternative to setTimeout as a way to insert events into the event queue. It is slightly more complicated to use, but its only real disadvantage is that it isn't as widely supported as setTimeout. It is supported in IE 8 and later and in browsers of the same vintage.

If you want to make use of the postMessage method and the message event for a zero delay addition to the event queue then the previous function can be rewritten as:

```
function computePiAsync() {
 var state = {};
 state.k = 0;
 state.pi = 0;
 window.addEventListener("message",computePi, false);
 function computePi() {
  if (state.k >= 100000000) return;
  var i;
  for (i = 0; i < 1000; i++) {
   state.k++;
   state.pi += 4 * Math.pow(-1, state.k + 1) / (2 * state.k - 1);
  }
  result.innerHTML = state.pi;
  count.innerHTML = state.k;
  window.postMessage("fireEvent", "*");
 }
 window.postMessage("fireEvent", "*");
}
```

You can use the same technique to turn nearly any long running computation into an asynchronous procedure.

All you have to do is break the computation down into small parts and preserve the state of the computation at the end of each chunk so that it can be restarted. Write the function so that it takes the state object and continues the computation.

This is always possible, even if the task isn't to sum a mathematical series.

For example, if you want to perform a complex database operation, simply save the point in the transaction that you have reached.

In most cases you will also need to include a callback so that the program using your function can make use of its results. This is not difficult to add, and a final version of the function complete with a callback parameter and a suitable callback function is:

```
computePiAsync(displayResult);

function displayResult(pi){
 result.innerHTML = pi;
}
function computePiAsync(callback) {
 var state = {};
 state.k = 0;
 state.pi = 0;
 window.addEventListener("message",computePi, false);
  function computePi() {
   if (state.k >= 10000000){
     callback(state.pi);
     return;
   };
   var i;
   for (i = 0; i < 1000; i++) {
     state.k++;
     state.pi += 4 * Math.pow(-1, state.k + 1) / (2 * state.k - 1);
   }
   window.postMessage("fireEvent", "*");
 }
 window.postMessage("fireEvent", "*");
}
```

Avoiding State – Yield

The big problem that we generally have to solve when splitting a computation up into small chunks is saving and restoring state. In general all you have to do is create a state object with all of the properties needed to restart the computation from where it left off. This is nearly always possible, but sometimes it requires a change to the code that isn't natural.

For example, the Pi computation is most naturally written:

```
 var pi = 0;
 var k;
 for (k = 1; k <= 100000; k++) {
  pi += 4 * Math.pow(-1, k + 1) / (2 * k – 1);
  result.innerHTML=pi;
  count.innerHTML=k;
 }
```

that is, with a single for loop repeating the iteration as many times as required. However, we can't use a for loop like this if the calculation is to be broken up into chunks. There is no way of pausing the for loop and restarting it where it left of – or rather there didn't used to be.

The yield keyword and generators were introduced in ES6 and are supported on all current browsers, but there is no legacy support – IE doesn't support it at all for example.

Yield and generators were introduced to allow JavaScript to create iterations in a natural way. A generator is a function that can contain a yield instruction. When a yield is encountered the function is suspended and optionally a value can be returned.

What is important for our particular use is that the function's state is automatically preserved by the system and you can restart the function from the yield instruction as if nothing had happened. This clearly provides us with an automatic way of preserving the state of a function that we want to divide up into chunks.

A simple example of generators and yield will be enough to explain its used in custom non-blocking functions. To use yield it has to be within a generator function which is declared in the same way as any function, but using a trailing asterisk:

```
function* myGenerator(){
}
```

You can write a generator function in the usual way, but with the added factor of being able to use yield to implement a return with the possibility of continuing.

For example a very simple generator is:

```
function* myGenerator(){
 yield 1;
 yield 2;
 yield 3;
}
```

The generator looks like a function that you could call to return one of the values, but things are a tiny bit more complicated. The generator is in fact an object factory. When you call it, it returns an object which will carry out the computation that you have specified.

That is:

```
var myNums=myGenerator();
```

doesn't compute the numbers in the body of the generator, but returns an object which will do the job. This object is stored in myNums and it has a single method, next, which you can think of as a "resume" command for the generator.

To get the first result of the generator we have to call the next method:

```
console.log(myNums.next().value);
```

The next method returns an object, an iteratorResult object, with two properties – value, which is the value passed by the yield, and done to indicate that the function has finished and cannot be resumed. You can see in the instruction above that the value 1 is printed to the console. That is, the next method runs the generator to the first yield which returns an iteratorResult object with value set to 1. The done property, were we to test it, is false. The function is now paused and can be resumed by another call to next:

```
console.log(myNums.next().value);
```

This starts the function off again at the instruction that follows the previous yield and so we see 2 printed in the console log. If you repeat this you would see 3 and then undefined, with done set to true.

The important point is that the yield preserves the state of the function which the next restores. This means we can use a for loop for example and expect its state to be preserved between yields:

```
function* myGenerator(){
  var i;
  for(i=1;i<4;i++){
    yield i;
  }
}
```

If you try this with the same console log statements then you will see 1,2,3, undefined.

The is more to say about the whole subject of generators and yield, but this is enough for us to write a version of the Pi program that makes use of the system to save its state. Notice that we can now use the natural for loop and we don't have to make any extra effort to break the program up or save state – we simply have to call yield at suitable intervals:

```
function* genComputePi() {
 var k;
 var pi = 0;
 for (k = 1; k <= 10000000; k++) {
  pi += 4 * Math.pow(-1, k + 1) / (2 * k - 1);
  if (Math.trunc(k / 1000) * 1000 === k) yield pi;
 }
 return pi;
}
```

The if statement checks to see if k is divisible by 1000 which results in yield being called every 1000 iterations.

Using this version of the function is slightly more difficult because we have to use the generator to create an iterator that we can call next on:

```
function computePiAsync() {
 var computePi = genComputePi();
 var pi;
 function resume() {
  pi = computePi.next();
  result.innerHTML = pi.value;
  if (!pi.done) setTimeout(resume, 0);
  return;
 }
 setTimeout(resume, 0);
 return;
}
```

Notice that apart from having to create computePi and make use of next to resume the function this is very like the way that we made use of setTimeout before – except we no longer have to save and use the state information – the system does this for us.

If you are using yield you might as well use postMessage instead of setTimeout as it is likely to be supported by any browser that supports yield:

```
function computePiAsync() {
 var computePi = genComputePi();
 var pi;
 window.addEventListener("message",resume, false);

 function resume() {
  pi = computePi.next();
  result.innerHTML = pi.value;
  if (!pi.done)
      window.postMessage("fireEvent", "*");
  return;
 }
 window.postMessage("fireEvent", "*");
 return;
}
```

Notice that in all of these cases closure is being used to allow the inner functions access to the variables of the outer functions.

Summary

- If you need to make your own long running functions non-blocking then you can either use another thread or split the computation into short sections.

- Threads are more powerful, but not all browsers support them and they can be difficult to implement.

- The basic idea in creating a non-blocking function without threads is to make them run in small chunks of time, releasing the UI thread often enough to keep the UI responsive.

- The main problem is is to keep the state of the computation so that it can be resumed after it has released the UI thread.

- In most cases you need to write the function using a state object to record the important information so that the function resumes from where it left off.

- To schedule the next run of the function you can use setTimeout or postMessage to place the function on the event queue.

- An alternative way to keep the state of the function is to write it as a generator and use the yield instruction to pause the function and next to resume it.

- If you use yield the system will look after the state for you and you can even pause for loops and generally write the function without having to worry about restoring state.

Chapter 5

Worker Threads

Until recently JavaScript has had no way to use any thread of execution other than the UI thread. For a language that was designed to work in an asynchronous event handling environment this is surprising. Today modern JavaScript does have additional threads and it is important to know how to use them.

The sort of asynchronous function we constructed in the previous chapter is more like simulated async rather than the real thing. It is simply a way of breaking up the execution into small chunks that release the UI thread to handle events before starting on the next chunk. This is not how the system provided non-blocking functions do the job. They generally start another thread of execution to do their allotted task and free the UI thread only to use it again when the task is complete and the callback has to be run.

This is ok for many purposes, but the lack of the ability to directly use another thread of execution is a limitation on what you can do easily in JavaScript.

Thus most asynchronous programming that occurs in practice is where another thread of execution is used to complete a long running task while the UI thread gets on with what it is supposed to do i.e. look after the UI.

For example, when you start an AJAX file download the operating system allocates another thread to look after the task. From the point of view of a JavaScript programmer it all seems magical. You ask for a file and some time later the file is available and all without the UI thread having to do anything at all. This is usually how we view asynchronous code in JavaScript, but behind the scenes the OS is busy scheduling threads.

There is also the very real possibility that the hardware supports multiple cores and the other thread might well be really running in parallel with the UI thread. That is, the OS can implement true parallel execution and this makes things work faster.

Until recently there was no way that a JavaScript programmer could take advantage of the OS to schedule threads or of multiple cores to implement true parallelism, but now we have the Web Worker which implements background processing on a non-UI thread.

This is also the basis of the Service worker facility that is used in the construction of progressive web apps – which are likely to be the next big thing in web app design. The Service Worker is the subject of Chapter Ten.

First we need to recap the basic principles of using a Web Worker.

Basic Web Worker

The good news is that Web Worker is very easy to use.

What is slightly difficult to get to grips with is working out what you are not allowed to do and achieving simple communication between the threads.

Ideally you should wrap any Web Worker tasks you create as Promises to make the code easier to use. We will take a look at how to do this in Chapter Seven – for the moment let's concentrate on using Web Workers raw.

There really is only one key object when using Web Workers, the Worker object.

The Worker object automatically starts a new thread and begins executing JavaScript code as soon as it is created.

The basic action is that it loads the JavaScript file that you specify in its constructor and starts the script executing on a new thread. It is possible to avoid using a separate file to store the code, but it is messy and best avoided. The reason the code is in a separate file is to keep the execution contexts separated on the threads. That is, the program that starts on the new Worker thread has no shared variables with the code that creates it.

So for example, if you have a program stored in myScript.js the instruction to run it is:

```
var worker=new Worker("myScript.js");
```

Although this is simple there is a subtlety that you need to get clear if you are to avoid making silly mistakes.

When you create a Worker object two things happen.

1. The code stored in myScript.js or whatever file you specify, is loaded and set running using a new OS level thread.

2. A Worker object is created on the UI thread and this is an object that your "standard" JavaScript code running on the UI thread can use to communicate with the new Worker thread.

If you think that this is obvious and doesn't need to be said, so much the better.

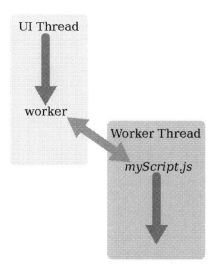

In the example given above worker is an object that exists on the UI thread and "myScript.js" loaded and running in isolation from the UI thread and the program that worker belongs to. Of course the Worker object provides methods that allow communication between the two programs and this is something we have to find out how to use.

If you need to load a library into the Worker thread's code you can use the importScripts function. You simply supply the URLs of the scripts to load as parameters. The scripts are downloaded in any order, but executed in the order you specify. The importScripts function is synchronous and blocks until all of the libraries have been downloaded.

Notice that you can try and load standard libraries into a Worker thread, but as the DOM is unavailable they might not work. For example jQuery certainly doesn't work as it needs the DOM to function.

The Trouble With Threads

If you have looked at the problem of writing multi-threaded programs, and all of the problems that this creates, this is where you might be getting worried.

In general multi-threaded programs are difficult to get right.

Starting a new thread so easily seems to be an easy way to do something dangerous. However, Web Workers have been implemented in a way that restricts the way that you use them to make them safe. At first these restrictions might seem tough to live with, but after a while you realize that they are perfectly reasonable and don't really stop you from doing anything.

The main simplification about threading with Web Workers is that the new thread cannot share anything with the UI thread.

The new thread cannot access any objects that the UI Thread can. This means it cannot interact with any global objects and it cannot interact with the DOM or the user interface in any way.

The Worker thread is isolated from the UI thread and cannot access any objects that are created by the UI thread and vice versa.

The new thread runs in a little world of its own, but don't panic as it can communicate with the UI thread in a very simple way.

This inability to share objects may seem a little restrictive, but it is a restriction that is necessary to make sure that the two threads you now have don't try to access the same object at the same time.

If this was allowed to happen you would need to introduce a lot of complicated machinery – locks, semaphores and so on – to make sure that the access was orderly and didn't give rise to any very difficult to find bugs – race conditions, deadlock and so on.

The problem is that if you have multiple threads accessing the same data you can't be sure of the order that things are happening in. Suppose one thread is in the middle of updating a shared object and a second thread deletes it in the middle of the update. This would at best create a program that didn't do what the user expected and at worst would generate a runtime error. The only way to stop this from happening is to use mechanisms that restrict access to shared objects so that only one thread can be working with it at any given time.

This is potentially very complex and very difficult to prove that you have things correct. The alternative to managing shared objects in this way is to ban shared objects. In this case there is absolutely no danger of a simultaneous access to any object, but this makes interaction impossible.

In other words the Web Worker has big restrictions so that you can use it without complication and without any danger.

For most purposes it is sufficient and hence very effective.

Web Workers do have access to all of the global core JavaScript objects that you might expect, but they are not shared.

They can also access some functions that are normally associated with the DOM – XMLHttpRequest() and setInterval etc.

The rule is that if the object is unique to the UI thread or could be shared in any way with the UI thread then you cannot get access to it and this is a condition that is obviously satisfied for all of the core JavaScript objects and the few DOM derived objects that are allowed.

To make up for this restriction there are two new objects that the Web Worker can access - WorkerNavigator and WorkerLocation. The navigator provides basic information about the app's context - the browser in use, appName, appVersion and so on. The location object provides details of where the app is in terms of the current URL.

If these two objects don't provide enough information you can easily arrange to pass the Worker thread additional data of your choosing.

Basic Communication Methods

So if the Web Worker is isolated from the UI thread, how do the two communicate?

The answer is that they both use events and a method that causes events on the other thread.

UI Thread To Worker Thread

Let's start with the UI thread sending a message to the Worker thread.

The Worker object that is created on the UI thread has a postMessage method which triggers a message event on the Worker thread. This is similar to the window.postMessage method that we have already used to implement custom events and asynchronous methods.

Notice that this is where the thread crossover occurs.

The Worker object is running on the UI thread, but the event occurs in the code running on the Worker thread. Notice that the Worker thread has an event queue all of its own – it is a complete event-driven program of its own.

For example:

```
var worker=new Worker("myScript.js");
worker.postMessage({mydata:"some data"});
```

The postMessage method triggers a message event in the worker code and sends it an event object that includes the data object as its data property. That is, event.data has a mydata property equal to "some data".

To get the message sent to the worker you have to set up an event handler and retrieve the event object's data property.

For example, in the Web Worker code you would write:

```
this.addEventListener("message", function (event) {
```

In the Web Worker code the global context is provided by this or self and this gives access to all of the methods and objects documented. To get the message you would use:

```
var somedata = event.data.mydata;
```

Of course as you are passing an object to the event handler you could package as many data items as you needed to.

Notice that it is important to be very clear what is going on here. The postMessage method call is on the UI thread, but the event handler is on the Worker thread.

It is also important to realize that the data that is passed between the two threads isn't shared.

A copy is made using the structured clone algorithm and it is this copy that the worker received. You can use a wide range of types of data to pass to the worker, but if it is big the time taken to copy could be significant.

If this is the case. you need to use a transferable object which is shared rather than copied – see later.

Worker Thread To UI Thread

Passing data from the Worker thread to the UI thread works in exactly the same way – only the other way round. You use the postMessage method of the DedicatedWorkerGlobalScope object in the Worker thread and attach an event handler for the message event in the UI thread. The DedicatedWorkerGlobalScope object can be accessed using this or self.

For example, in the Worker code:

```
this.postMessage({mydata:"some data"});
```

or

```
self.postMessage({mydata:"some data"});
```

notice that in this case you can use this or self to call postMessage because you are running inside the Web Worker.

This triggers a message event in the UI thread and you can define a handler and retrieve the data using:

```
worker.addEventListener("message",
  function (e) {
    var somedata= e.data.mydata;
  });
```

Once again you have to be very clear that you understand what is running where. In this case the postMessage method is running on the Worker thread and the event handler is running on the UI thread.

This is about all there is to using Web Workers.

There are some details about error handling and terminating the thread before it is complete, but these are just details. The general idea is that you use the message event to communicate between the two threads.

There is one subtle point that is worth keeping in mind. The events that you trigger in passing data between the two threads will happen in the order that you trigger them, but they may not be handled promptly.

For example, if you start your Worker thread doing an intensive calculation then triggering a "*how are you doing*" message event from the UI thread might not work as you expect. It could be that the Worker thread is so occupied with its task that events are ignored until it reaches the end. The same happens with the messages passed from the Worker thread, but in this case the UI thread is generally not so focused on one task and so events usually get processed.

The rule is that UI thread events are generally handled promptly because that's the way we tend to build UI code, but Worker thread events aren't because that's the way we tend to build Worker code.

That is, events going from the Worker thread to the UI get processed as part of keeping the UI responsive. Events going the other way, i.e. from the UI thread to the Worker, are not so reliable. If you want to drive the Worker thread using events from the UI thread you basically have to design it to be event driven. This means writing the Worker thread as an event handler that responds to the messages that the UI thread sends.

A Simple Web Worker Example

As an example let's use the calculation of Pi example again.

First we need a new JavaScript file called pi.js containing the following code:

```
var state = {};
state.k = 0;
state.pi = 0;
var i;
for (i = 0; i < 10000000; i++) {
    state.k++;
    state.pi += 4 * Math.pow(-1, state.k + 1) / (2 * state.k - 1);
}
this.postMessage(state);
```

You can see that this worker is just a simple modification to the earlier program. The most important change is that we now no longer need to break the calculation up into chunks. As it is being performed on a separate thread it can run to completion and take as much time at it likes without any fear of blocking the UI – which is running on a different thread.

When the calculation is complete it uses the postMessage method to fire a "message" event on the UI thread and supply the result. Notice that we can pass as much data back to the UI thread as we like using an object.

The UI thread code is simply:

```
button1.addEventListener("click" ,
 function (event) {
  button1.setAttribute("disabled", true);
  var worker = new Worker("pi.js");
  worker.addEventListener("message",
    function (event) {
       result.innerHTML=event.data.pi;
       count.innerHTML=event.data.k;
       button.setAttribute("disabled", false); }
  );
});
```

Where we are using the UI of the previous examples. When the button is clicked the Worker constructor loads pi.js and starts it running on a new thread. The constructor returns a Worker object which runs on the UI thread in the variable worker.

When the Worker thread is finished it fires the "message" event which is handled by the anonymous function which displays the result.

This is a very typical use of Worker threads. The UI thread generally sends some data to initialize the Worker thread and then simply waits for message events. Notice that the button is disabled when the Worker thread has been started so as to avoid starting multiple Worker threads. There is nothing wrong with this if you actually want to start multiple threads, but it is easy to do so simply by accident unless you take steps to stop it happening.

If you try the program out you will find that on most modern hardware it is faster than the custom async version in the previous chapter. Using multiple threads is generally faster because it uses the hardware and any idle time more efficiently than using the event queue.

Periodic Updates – The Event Problem

There is nothing stopping you from adding a periodic update to the Worker thread so that the UI thread displays the progress of the calculation. You might think that all you have to do is setup a periodic event using setTimeout or setInterval something like:

```
var state = {};
state.k = 0;
state.pi = 0;
var i;
setInterval(this.postMessage(state),1000);
for (i = 0; i < 100000000; i++) {
    state.k++;
    state.pi += 4 * Math.pow(-1, state.k + 1) / (2 * state.k - 1);
}
this.postMessage(state);
```

Notice that the setInterval fires an event every 1000 ms i.e. every second that the UI will process and display the status. If you try it you will discover that it doesn't work. The reason is very obvious once you notice that the Worker thread is fully occupied when the one second events occur and so they remain in the worker's event queue. Notice that it is the Worker thread that processes the worker's event queue. The periodic updates occur all at once when the calculation is over and continue to happen from then on.

If the Worker thread is occupied with a computation then it can't service the event queue.

This is exactly the same problem we had with the event-driven UI thread and it is the problem with all event-driven threads – they have to be doing nothing to respond to events.

We could use the techniques we used to break up the calculation in the UI thread, but this would lose us some of the advantage of using a Worker thread. You might think that the solution is to use yet another Worker thread just to service the regular events, but the problem here is that another Worker thread would not have access to the status object.

The simplest solution is to include a timer in the loop that does the calculation and use it to fire the message event:

```
var state = {};
state.k = 0;
state.pi = 0;
var i;
var time=Date.now();
for (i = 0; i < 100000000; i++) {
    if(Date.now()-time>1000){
        this.postMessage(state);
        time=Date.now();
    }
    state.k++;
    state.pi += 4 * Math.pow(-1, state.k + 1) / (2 * state.k - 1);
}
this.postMessage(state);
```

This works, but testing the time every iteration is inefficient. However, attempts to make it more efficient are not easy.

Controlling The Worker

As we have just seen the fundamental problem in making good use of Worker threads is that they make use of an event-driven architecture just like the UI thread, but they are far less suited to it. Sometimes events are natural for the task. For example, a Worker thread that manages downloads or database interactions is going to be idle waiting for the task to complete for enough of the time for the thread to service the event queue. Other computationally intensive tasks are less suited to events.

61

If you are familiar with other languages you may have used commands to start, stop and put the thread to sleep for a given number of milliseconds. There are no such features in JavaScript because the additional threads that you create are always event driven. You do not pause or sleep a Worker thread because if you don't have something for it to do then it looks after the event queue i.e. it runs its own dispatcher.

The closest you can get to pausing the thread is to make a call to setInterval to restart a function after a few milliseconds and then perform a return to free the thread. This is of course exactly the technique we would use for the UI thread.

You can stop the thread, however, and this is about the only control you have and it is a very coarse one as it stops the thread without any warning or time to finish what it is doing. To stop a Worker thread in this way all you have to do is call the terminate method on the Worker object:

```
worker.terminate();
```

What if the Worker thread wants to terminate itself?

You might think that executing a return or just finishing the main program of the Worker thread would be enough to stop it, but of course it doesn't. It simply frees the thread to service the event queue. If you want to terminate the thread you have to use the close method:

```
close();
```

This places the thread into a "close mode" where it doesn't respond to any events. Your code continues to run until the thread is freed. The previous example should have terminated the thread:

```
this.postMessage(state);
close();
```

The only other sort of control that is available is to respond to an error condition. If the Worker thread throws an exception then it has a chance to handle its own error event. If it doesn't then the error event is passed to the thread that created the worker where it can be handled and canceled.

The Async Worker Thread

If you want to control a Worker thread more finely than terminate allows or if you want to sent the Worker thread state messages you have no choice but to make it fully asynchronous. This means treat it like the UI thread and never block the thread or monopolize it.

If you see the Worker thread as your way of being free from the concerns of asynchronous code then you are going to be disappointed.

If you want your Worker thread to be responsive to the outside world e.g. the UI thread, then you have to implement asynchronous code and specifically you have to give up the thread at regular intervals so that the event queue can be serviced and messages from the UI thread or from the timer can be handled.

What this means in practice is that you have to break up any long running function in the Worker thread. You can use yield to save the state of the function as a browser that supports Worker threads is likely to support generators, but you can't use the postMessage window method because there is no window object in a Worker thread. This means you need to use setTimeout to restart the function.

For example, let's change the Pi computation so that the UI thread can start it, stop it and ask for an update. Notice that in this case it is the UI thread that asks for the update and not the Worker thread that decides to supply one.

First we need to implement the genComputPi function which is exactly the same as the one used in the UI thread when yield was used to save the state:

```
function* genComputePi() {
    var k;
    var pi = 0;
    for (k = 1; k <= 1000000; k++) {
        pi += 4 * Math.pow(-1, k + 1) / (2 * k - 1);
        if (Math.trunc(k / 1000) * 1000 === k)
            yield pi;
    }
    return pi;
}
```

The computePiAsync is a little different in that it now has to restart the computePi function or post the final value back to the UI thread when the computation is complete:

```
function computePiAsync() {
    var computePi = genComputePi();
    function resume() {
        pi = computePi.next();
        if (!pi.done)
            setTimeout(resume, 0);
        if (pi.done)
            postMessage(pi);
        return;
    }
    setTimeout(resume, 0);
    return;
}
```

The biggest change is that now we need a controller function to respond to the message events from the UI Thread:

```
var pi;
this.addEventListener("message", function (event) {
    switch (event.data) {
        case "start":
            computePiAsync();
            break;
        case "update":
            postMessage(pi);
            break;
        case "stop":
            close();
            break;
    }
});
```

This controller function is called whenever the UI thread sends the worker a message with a string Object. It then works out what the message is and performs the action.

If the string is "start" it runs the computation which releases the thread every 1000 iterations so that the event queue is given a chance to process another message.

If the string is "update" then it simply posts a message back with the current value of pi. Notice that for this to work pi has to be global. An alternative to making pi global is to wrap the entire code in a function which is immediately executed, meaning any variable will be made available to all of the functions because of closure.

Finally if the string is "stop" it stops the Worker thread. In general the response to stop could be more sophisticated and include preserving state before the thread was terminated.

The UI thread now has to "drive" the Worker thread by posting messages to it. First it has to set things up including the event handler for the response to the update command:

```
var worker = new Worker("pi.js");
worker.addEventListener("message",
        function (event) {
            result.innerHTML=event.data.value;
        }
);
```

To control the Worker thread we now have to send some messages:

```
worker.postMessage("start");
setInterval(function(){
            worker.postMessage("update");
        },100);
```

The start message sets the computation off and every 100 milliseconds an update is requested. Notice that if you ask for an update more often than the computation yields then the update events accumulate. All of the pending updates will be performed before the calculation resumes, but the repeats are going to be a waste of time. It is important not to issue messages much faster than the receiving event queue can deal with them.

The general idea is the same for all Worker threads that need to be controlled from the UI thread.

1. Make sure that all long running functions in the Worker thread yield frequently.

2. Make sure that all functions in the Worker thread that yield are restarted using setTimeout or similar.

3. Write a controller function that responds to the message event in the Worker thread that determines what to do next.

4. The controlling thread has to send message to the Worker thread to make it do what it has to.

Running a Worker Without a Separate File

Some times it is desirable to include the code for a Worker thread in the same file as say the UI Thread code or even the HTML page itself. This can be done as a special case of using a Blob and a Data URL. It is a special case because generally a Blob can represent anything that you can put in a file, and a Data URL can provide a URL to the Blob.

So all we have to do is put the code that would have gone into the file into a Blob, generate a Data URL for the Blob, and pass this to the worker's constructor.

If you have a string, workerCodeString say, which has all of the code you want to execute then implementing this is easy:

```
var blob = new Blob([workerCodeString],
                         {type: 'application/javascript'});
var url = URL.createObjectURL(blob);
var worker = new Worker(url);
```

The Blob constructor takes an array of strings that it concatenates to make the "file". The second parameter, the options object, is used to specify the file type using the same MIME type you would specify in a full <Script> tag loading the JavaScript. The blob can now be considered to be an in-memory version of the file holding the JavaScript. We now generate a Data URL for the blob and use it to create the worker.

The only part of this procedure that is difficult is getting the code into the workerCodeString String. Getting a multi-line string complete with any

65

escape characters into a JavaScript variable isn't easy. Fortunately there is an easier way.

If you take all of the code that was in the separate JavaScript file and surround it by a function declaration:

```
function workerCode(){
  all the code that would have gone in the file
  completely unmodified
}
```

Notice that you put all of the code into the function ignoring the fact it is within a function. Next you can get a string version of the code using the workerCode function's toString() method. So we can get the String we need using:

```
var workerCodeString = workerCode.toString();
```

Almost, but not quite. We don't want the workerCode string in the Worker thread we want all of the code that is defined within it so we use the usual trick of immediately executing the workerCode function by wrapping it in () and following it with () to execute it:

```
var workerCodeString = "(" + workerCode.toString() + ")()";
```

Now when the thread receives the code it will immediately execute the function and all of the code it contains will be either executed or added to the global environment. Notice that top level variables declared in the code aren't global, but are accessible to all of the functions due to closure.

This is a completely general procedure.

1. Create a function workerCode or whatever you want to call it.
2. Write your thread code within the workerCode function as if it was executing at the global level.
3. Get the code into a string using workerCode.toString(), but wrap it in () and follow it by (). That is "("+workerCode.toString()+")();".
4. Convert the String to a Blob.
5. Get the Data URL of the Blob.
6. Pass the Data URL to the Worker constructor.

For example the previous pi computation can be loaded directly from the same file as the UI thread using:

```
var workerCodeString = "(" + workerCode.toString() + ")()";
var blob = new Blob([workerCodeString],
                              {type: 'application/javascript'});
var url = URL.createObjectURL(blob);
var worker = new Worker(url);

worker.addEventListener("message",
    function (event) {
        result.innerHTML = event.data.value;
 } );

worker.postMessage("start");
setInterval(function(){
        worker.postMessage("update");
     },100);}

function workerCode() {
 var pi = 0;
 this.addEventListener("message", function (event) {
    switch (event.data) {
        case "start":
            computePiAsync();
            break;
        case "update":
            postMessage(pi);
            break;
        case "stop":
            close();
            break;
    }
});
 function computePiAsync() {
    var computePi = genComputePi();
    function resume() {
        pi = computePi.next();
        if (!pi.done)
            setTimeout(resume, 0);
        if (pi.done)
            postMessage(pi);
        return;
    }
    setTimeout(resume, 0);
    return;
 }
```

```
function* genComputePi() {
    var k;
    var pi = 0;
    for (k = 1; k <= 1000000; k++) {
        pi += 4 * Math.pow(-1, k + 1) / (2 * k - 1);
        if (Math.trunc(k / 1000) * 1000 === k)
            yield pi;
    }
    return pi;
}
}
```

Transferable Objects

The way that Worker threads avoid many of the problems of multi-threading is by limiting the way threads can interact. They can only communicate by sending messages and, in particular, any data that is included in the message isn't shared, but copied. This means that each thread is always working on its own data and no object can be used by more than one thread at a time.

Copying data is safe, but if the data is large it can be slow. An alternative is to use transferable objects. These are not copied, but only one thread can access them at any given time. The idea is that the object belongs to just one thread and only that thread can access the object. Ownership of the thread can be passed to another thread by the object being included in a message sent from the current owner to another thread.

Transferable objects are only supported in the latest browsers and to a limited extent in IE 10 so they need to be used with caution. The mechanism only applies to three types of object - ArrayBuffer, MessagePort and ImageBitMap. This makes sense because these are all potentially large objects which are best not passed by copy.

To send a transferable object you simply follow the usual data object in postMessage by an array of transferable objects – IE10 is limited to a single object.

The way that transferable objects work is simple, but it can be confusing.

You pass data using the message object as usual which becomes the data property of the event object passed to the event handler. The data that you want to transfer has to be included either as the message object or a property of the message object. To be passed by transfer rather then clone the object also has to be listed in the transfer array.

So for example:

```
sendMessage(object,[object]);
```

will transfer object and the event handler will receive the objects as event.data.

Alternatively you could use:

```
sendMessage({mydata: object},[object]);
```

which will also transfer the object, but the event handler will receive it as event.data.mydata. Obviously you could pass additional properties and if these were not included in the transfer list they would be passed by cloning.

Once an object has been transferred it is no longer usable in the original thread. For example in the case of an ArrayBuffer its size is reduced to zero. Notice that once transferred its ownership cannot be simply transferred back because the reference that is passed is in event.data or event.data.myobject and not the original reference. That is, it is not a simple turning off and on of the original reference. You can arrange for this to happen, however.

We need a very simple example and to do this we need to work with an ArrayBuffer. An ArrayBuffer is a raw collection of bytes and you cannot access it directly. It has to be converted into a typed array before you can access its data.

However, we can simply create a raw buffer and pass it back and forth between the main thread and the worker thread as an example without worrying about what data it contains:

```
var worker = new Worker("transfer.js");
var arrayBuf = new ArrayBuffer(8);
console.log("UI before transfer " + arrayBuf.byteLength);
worker.postMessage(arrayBuf, [arrayBuf]);
console.log("UI after transfer" + arrayBuf.byteLength);
```

This simply creates an eight byte ArrayBuffer and transfers it to the Worker thread. When the program is run you see:

```
UI before transfer 8
UI after transfer 0
```

Indicating that the ArrayBuffer is no longer available in the UI thread.

In the Worker thread we can use the ArrayBuffer in the standard way:

```
this.addEventListener("message",
      function(event){
       console.log("Worker got data! " + event.data.byteLength);
      });
```

And you will see the message:

```
Worker got data! 8
```

Indicating that the ArrayBuffer is now available in the Worker thread.

The Worker can pass the ArrayBuffer back to the UI thread:

```
this.addEventListener("message",function(event){
    console.log("Worker got data! " + event.data.byteLength);
    postMessage(event.data,[event.data]);
    console.log("Worker sent data! " + event.data.byteLength);
});
```

After the data has been transferred back to the UI thread you once again will see that the length of the ArrayBuffer is zero.

In the UI thread the data can be retrieved in the usual way:

```
worker.addEventListener("message",
    function (event) {
      console.log("UI after return " + event.data.byteLength);
      console.log("UI after return original " + arrayBuf.byteLength);
    });
```

In this case you will see that the event.data is an ArrayBuffer of eight bytes and the original arrayBuf is still zero – that is the original transferred data is not restored.

You can, of course, restore the reference to the original data:

```
worker.addEventListener("message",
    function (event) {
      console.log("UI after return " + event.data.byteLength);
      arrayBuf=event.data;
      console.log("UI after return original " + arrayBuf.byteLength);
    });
```

Now it looks as if the original data has been handed back by the Worker thread.

The big problem with transferring data is that the thread that owned it originally doesn't get the use of it, not even a copy, while the other thread is using it. This doesn't matter as long as the initial owner is generating the data for the first time. For example, if a Worker thread is downloading a resource it can transfer it to the UI thread to be used with no problems. Compare this to a Worker thread that is modifying rather than originating the data. If the UI thread passes the Worker thread a bitmap to process, what does the UI thread show while the worker has ownership?

At the time of writing support for ImageBitmap is restricted to Firefox and Chrome and is best avoided.

Shared and Service Workers

There are other types of Worker object that you can use, but these are more specialized and not as well supported. In particular, Safari dropped support to both Shared and Service workers.

A SharedWorker is another thread that can be accessed from multiple browsing contexts – windows, iframes or other workers. You create a shared worker using:

```
var worker=new SharedWorker(url);
```

Communication is via postMessage as per a standard Worker thread, but now we have to use a port object to make the connection. You have to start the port and then you use its postMessage method:

```
worker.port.start();
worker.port.sendMessage(data);
```

The connection from the SharedWorker back to the UI thread is performed via the onconnect event:

```
this.addEventListener("onconnect",function(event){
 var port=e.ports[0];
...
```

Once you have the port object you can send messages using it:

```
port.start();
port.sendMessage(data);
```

Apart from the need to use a port object to send messages, the only other difference is that a single instance of the Worker code serves all of the other threads making use of it. To take advantage of a Shared Worker's abilities you really need to store the port object as different threads connect to it. By keeping a list of ports, the SharedWorker can pass data from one thread to another and hence one window or iFrame to another. Notice that the one origin rule applies to SharedWorkers and all code and windows have to have come from the same source domain.

SharedWorkers are interesting, but until Apple decides to support them they are probably not a good gamble. ServiceWorkers on the other hand might be. They provide facilities that make the offline experience of using a web app much more like that of a native app. As such some see the ServiceWorker as the future of the web. At first Apple withdrew support for ServiceWorkers in Safari, but it is currently under consideration. The final chapter is devoted to using ServiceWorkers.

Summary

- You can create a Worker object which runs on a different thread to the UI thread.

- The UI thread doesn't share any objects with the new thread and vice versa.

- The Worker thread has access to all of JavaScript and a subset of the global objects available to the UI thread.

- Communication from the thread that created the Worker object to the new thread makes use of its postMessage method.

- Communication from the Worker thread to the thread that created it also makes use of the postMesssage method, but of the DedicatedWorkerGlobalScope object.

- In each case a message event is triggered on the appropriate thread and the data property of the event object provides the data sent as part of the message.

- The data transferred to the worker thread and to the UI thread is a copy, a clone, of the original.

- By limiting the way the thread can interact, the JavaScript programmer is protected from the main difficulties of multi-threading and we don't have to worry about locks and race conditions.

- A big problem with using Worker threads is that communication is event driven, but the Worker thread is at its most simple when just ignoring asynchronous considerations and just gets on with the job.

- To allow for responsive communication between the threads both have to be written in an asynchronous style. Any long running function in the Worker thread will mean that it doesn't respond to messages sent to it from the UI thread.

- You can use a Blob object and a Data URL to avoid having to use a separate file for the Worker's code.

- A faster way to exchange data between threads is to use transferable objects.

- As well as dedicated Workers you can also create SharedWorkers which can pass messages between different threads and ServiceWorkers which make implementing web apps easier. Neither are supported by Safari.

Chapter 6

Consuming Promises

Promises are a way of organizing asynchronous calls that is better than using callbacks. The callbacks are still there, but they come with a degree of organization. Promises are also the basis for the next level of making async code easier to write – async and await.

In this chapter we are going to look at using Promises to create asynchronous code that is easy to understand and hard for bugs to hide in. Specifically we are going to look at how to use the Promises that other functions return in place of callbacks.

That is we are going to be looking at consuming Promises.

In the next chapter we will look at how to add Promise support to your own asynchronous code i.e. how to produce Promises for others to use.

What is the problem?

As should be perfectly clear by now the problem is that JavaScript is single-threaded and this means if you were to call any functions that need to wait while some external event occurs – a file to download say – then, for the duration of the event, your app would appear to freeze. The user interface, and events in particular, are all handled by the same thread and if that thread is in a wait state then nothing else gets done.

The usual solution to this problem as explained in earlier chapters is to use a callback function. The callback is passed to the function that is going to do the long job and instead of keeping the thread waiting it simply returns immediately. This allows the thread to do other work while it get on with its task. When it has finished it calls the callback function, usually with the result of the task. The callback function then processes the results.

Callbacks are difficult because they alter the flow of control in an unnatural way and this has been explained in an earlier chapter. However, it is worth saying that the precise problem that Promises were introduced to solve is that of running asynchronous tasks one after the other.

That is, if you have three asynchronous tasks and simply call them:

```
TaskA();
TaskB();
TaskC();
```

Then they will execute in an order that depends on how long each takes. They effectively run in parallel.

If you want them to run sequentially – that is TaskB only starts after TaskA ends, and TaskC starts after TaskB ends, then you have to use some sort of mechanisms to signal the end of each task and initiate the next one in the sequence. We looked at some ways of doing this in Chapter 3, but the most basic is to use callbacks.

The callback solution is to use nested callbacks. Something like:

```
TaskA(callBackTaskB(callBackTaskC)));
```

where each task accepts a callback that is invoked when it ends. This looks simple enough in this example, but this is because it is over simplified. In real life nested callbacks quickly degenerate into "callback hell" and there is no standard way of handling errors except for having a success and a failure callback for each function.

Running asynchronous tasks sequentially is something Promises make easy.

Promises are an approach to the whole problem of working with asynchronous functions and as such they are worth knowing about.

Let's look first at the basic operation of a Promise.

The Basic Promise

An operation that takes some time will generally return a Promise object at once and then complete its task in the background:

```
var mypromise=slowFun(args);
```

Notice that even though you get a Promise object returned at once, it is unlikely that slowFun has finished whatever it is trying to do when the program moves on to the next instruction. Indeed the whole program might have come to an end before slowFun finishes.

There is also the idea that the slow function is computing a value which your program is waiting for – this isn't necessarily the case as you could be just waiting for it to complete what it is doing. However, in most cases the Promise is regarded as being a Promise to deliver a future value and this view is often helpful.

What do you do with a Promise?

The most common thing to do is to use its then method to set up what should happen when the slow function is complete:

```
mypromise.then(onComplete,onError);
```

where onComplete is a function that is called when the slow function finishes its task. It is passed the value that the slow function generates on completion. That is, when the Promise is fulfilled it supplies the value to the onComplete.

The onError function is optional and is called if an error occurs while the slow function is executing. The value that the onError receives is the reason for the error.

Both the onComplete and onError functions are optional.

A Promise object is in one of three states.

- ◆ When it is first created it is **pending**.
- ◆ If the task ends correctly then it is in the **resolved** or **fulfilled** state.
- ◆ If the task ends with an error it enters the **rejected** state.

A Promise is also said to be **settled** if it isn't pending i.e. if it is either fulfilled or rejected.

Once a Promise is settled its state and value don't change.

It is important to realize that there is no rush to use the then method, or any other method to define the functions to be called. The Promise object's state determines if and when any of the functions are called. If a Promise is already settled when you add functions as part of a then method they will still be carried out.

The key idea is that a Promise always activates the onComplete or onError after the code that is currently running has finished.

That is, a Promise always executes its functions asynchronously.

Understanding of this is essential to your understanding and use of Promises. You can be assured that nothing will happen as the result of you creating or modifying a Promise until the current thread of execution has been released. In particular, no onComplete or onError functions will be called, and as a result there is no possibility of any "race" conditions occurring. The Promise will resolve and call the functions you have specified perhaps long after your code has performed a return.

In particular, you can add as many onComplete or onError functions as you want to. For example:

```
mypromise.then(onComplete1,onError1);
mypromise.then(onComplete2,onError2);
```

When the Promise is settled, the handlers are not necessarily called in the order that they were added.

A Demonstration Promise

One of the problems with explaining how to use Promises is that core JavaScript doesn't make any use of them. All of the standard JavaScript functions were defined well before Promises were invented and none of them return a Promise by default. Fortunately it is very easy to wrap them so that they do return a Promise, and this is part of the topic of the next chapter which demonstrates how to use Promises in your own custom functions.

Promises are used in most modern libraries such as jQuery, but to avoid having to install, use and explain a library simply to have some real function to demonstrate how Promises work, it is easier to present a small example program:

```
function delay(t, p) {
 var promise = new Promise(
   function (resolve, reject) {
     setTimeout(function () {
                 var r = Math.random();
                 if (r > p) {
                    resolve(r);
                 } else {
                    reject(r);
                 }
             }, t);
  });
 return promise;
}
```

This function makes use of setTimeout to create a non-blocking asynchronous function that returns a Promise which resolves after t milliseconds. The second parameter determines the probability that the Promise will be rejected. You can set p equal to zero for a Promise that always succeeds, and to one for a Promise that always fails. The function returns the random number generated as its result to the Promise.

You could say that delay returns an asynchronous random number.

Don't worry how this function works at the moment, it is explained in the next chapter. For now all that matters is that you can use it to try out Promises in action.

Let's see how it can be used in the simplest of ways:

```
var promise = delay(1000, 0.5);
promise.then(
            function () {
              console.log("success ");
            },
            function () {
              console.log("fail ");
            });
```

The call to delay starts the timer and returns a Promise at once. Notice that even if the timer finishes nothing can happen until the program releases the UI thread to service the event queue. The Promise object has onComplete and onReject functions defined. If you run the program you will see "success" or "fail" about 50% of the time each.

Of course you can retrieve the value that the Promise returns:

```
var promise = delay(1000, 0.5);
promise.then(
            function (r) {
              console.log("success "+r);
            },
            function (r) {
              console.log("fail "+r);
            });
```

You can only return a single value, but, of course, that value can be an object and so can return as much data as you want to pack into it.

If you don't want to use the Promise any further there is no need to save a reference to the Promise object that is returned you could just write:

```
delay(1000, 0.5).then(
            function (r) {
              console.log("success "+r);
            },
            function (r) {
              console.log("fail "+r);
            });
```

and this is indeed the most common Promise idiom.

At this point you might wonder what Promises have to offer over callbacks?

It is true that at this stage a Promise is very little different from a callback. The only real advantage is that it provides a standard way of setting up callbacks and the ability to set these up at any point in the program as opposed to only where the asynchronous function is called.

If this was the only advantage to using Promises we probably wouldn't bother, but a small addition to their behavior has a big effect.

Chaining Promises

At the moment it looks as if a Promise is just another way to write callbacks. After all what is the difference between writing:

```
slowFun(args,successCallback,errorCallback);
```

and:

```
slowFun(args).then(successCallback,errorCallback);
```

Looked at in this way there is no real difference and if it helps you understand the way Promises work then by all means think about them as just another way to write callbacks. However, there is a little more sophistication here than you might think and its all to do with the idiom of chaining functions.

Promises can be chained and this provides a way to run asynchronous functions sequentially.

A particular problem with asynchronous tasks is to arrange that taskB is only started when taskA has completed. In Chapter Three we looked at various ways of achieving this including the use of a queue. Promises provide yet another and arguably the best way of doing this.

If you want to perform two asynchronous tasks, one after the other, you can by simply chaining the method calls. As in all function chaining to make it work you have to return the correct sort of object from each function and in this case its another Promise.

To understand what is going on we need to master one subtle point of the way Promises work.

The then method always immediately returns a Promise object that is settled when the original Promise is.

You can think of this as a Promise linked to the onComplete or onError function specified in the then. The value of the Promise is the value that the function returns. The way that this behaves can seem complicated so we will introduce the ideas in stages – with an overview at the end.

You can use this new Promise to set up its callbacks as its onComplete and onError functions. In its turn this use of them will return a Promise that is linked to the new onComplete function and its value.

What all of this means is that by chaining Promises you can build a queue of onComplete/onError functions which will be executed sequentially in the order given by the chaining. This is very similar to the controller object introduced in Chapter Three which created a queue of functions to call. In this case it is the chain of Promises each linked to the previous Promise which forms the queue.

For example:

```
var myPromise1 = delay(1000, 0);
var myPromise2=myPromise1.then(
                        function (value) {
                          console.log(value);
                          return "Hello";
                        });
myPromise2.then(
                function (value) {
                  console.log(value);
                });
```

The delay function returns a Promise object which we can use to set an onComplete using then. However, then also returns a Promise object which can have an onComplete which will be called when it is resolved.

Notice that the first function we use, i.e. delay, is slightly different from the rest in that it returns the Promise that starts the chain and it isn't executed within a then.

The value of each Promise in the chain is whatever the previous onComplete/onError returns.

If you run this you will see the random number produced by delay followed by "Hello" displayed in the console.

It is important that you really understand this example.

The key is to realize that myPromise1 and myPromise2 are returned at once by the delay and the then. This is always the case because it is what allows the code to continue executing and run to completion.

At some time in the future after the code has completed the delay finishes and myPromise1 is fulfilled and the onComplete function is fired with the Promise's value i.e. the random number. It then returns "Hello" which is the value that myPromise2 has been waiting for and it calls its onComplete function.

Of course this isn't how this code would generally be written, but it does help you to see each of the Promises in the chain.

You can write it more usually using the chaining or fluent style:

```
delay(1000, 0).then(
            function (value) {
             console.log(value);
             return "Hello";
            })
         .then(
            function (value) {
             console.log(value);
            });
```

This is neater and more compact, but it is harder to see what Promise objects are in play.

Returning a Promise

So far we have been chaining together synchronous functions that return their final value quickly enough for it not to be a problem. The only asynchronous function involved in the chain has been the first one that returned the Promise that started the chain off.

If we include a non-blocking asynchronous function in the chain then it should, if it is playing fair, return a Promise so as not to hold everything up. This is where the Promise chain becomes really useful.

The rule is that if an onComplete function returns a value then this value is used as the resolved value of the Promise that the then creates. However, if an onComplete function returns a Promise then the Promise that the then creates has to wait for the first Promise to resolve.

This behavior means that the chain of function calls will execute sequentially even if it contains non-blocking asynchronous functions as long as they return a Promise.

For example, suppose one of the then functions was another call to delay:

```
var myPromise1 = delay(1000, 0);
var myPromise2=myPromise1.then(
                    function (value) {
                      console.log(value);
                      return delay(500,0);
                    });
 myPromise2.then(
            function (value) {
                console.log(value);
            });
```

What happens is almost identical to the previous example.

The first delay starts the timer and then immediately returns myPromise1. Next the then immediately returns myPromise2 and sets up the onComplete callback so that it calls delay and returns its result which is a Promise.

The code then comes to an end freeing up the UI thread. At some time later delay finishes and this resolves myPromise1 with a value equal to the random number. This causes the onComplete to start running which prints the value and starts the second delay.

The second delay immediately returns a Promise which is pending, i.e unresolved. MyPromise2 continues to wait because the Promise it has been supplied with is unresolved. MyPromise2 can only resolve if the supplied Promise is resolved, they are both waiting on the value to become available.

Eventually the second delay ends and the Promise returned is resolved and this provides a value for MyPromise2 and it too is resolved. Finally MyPromise2's onComplete is called and displays the value i.e. the second random value.

What happens when a Promise is returned to a Promise is the trickiest part of understanding Promises, but if you think of a simple Promise as waiting for a value to be available, then a Promise that is waiting for a Promise is waiting for the same final value:

```
promise1 -waiting> promise2 -waiting> value
```

when promise2 gets the value it resolves and passes the value back to promise1 which is also resolved. The principle extends to more than two Promises and you can have a chain of Promises all waiting for the final one in the chain to resolve.

Without using Promises the only way to make sure that asynchronous functions occur one after another is to nest callbacks, or you could use a function queue as described in Chapter Three.

It all depends on two properties of Promises:

◆ then returns a Promise on the value returned by its onComplete or onError function

and

◆ a Promise that is returned a value that is another Promise only resolves when the returned Promise does.

Chaining Promises is a fundamental way to order asynchronous tasks.

This is to be preferred to the alternative of nested Promises which is the Promise analog of nesting callbacks e.g.:

```
delay(1000, 0).then(
            function (value) {
                console.log(value);
                delay(500,0).then(
                  function (value) {
                    console.log(value);
                  });
            });
```

This nests a callback within a callback. It is better to return the Promise object and write things like:

```
object.then(oncomplete1).then(oncomplete2)
```

and so on.

The important point is:

◆ if you chain Promises or asynchronous functions using then they are executed sequentially.

Notice that to get things to happen in parallel you have to avoid chaining. For example to run two delays at the same time you would use:

```
delay(1000,0).then(
        function (value) {
          console.log(value);

        });
 delay(500,0).then(
        function (value) {
          console.log(value);
        })
```

Notice – no chaining.

Also notice that if you want to add additional handlers to the same Promise you can't use chaining.

That is:

```
mypromise.then(onComplete1);
mypromise.then(onComplete2);
```

adds onComplete1 and onComplete2 to mypromise so that they will be executed when it is fulfilled. Both onComplete functions are passed the value of mypromise i.e. the same value.

However:

```
mypromise.then(onComplete1).then(onComplete2);
```

seems to do the same thing, but onComplete1 is called by mypromise with its value and onComplete2 is called by the Promise returned by the then and its value is whatever onComplete1 returns.

Using Named Functions

There is a tendency in JavaScript to always use anonymous functions because they seem to fit in with the flow of control you are trying to express.

Hence it is typical to write:

```
delay(1000,0.5)
  .then(
    function (value) {
      console.log(value);
      return delay(500,0.5);
    },
    function(error){
     handle the error
    })
  .then(
    function (value) {
     console.log(value);
    },
    function(error){
     handle the error
    });
```

However, there are significant downsides to using anonymous functions. In particular, error reporting doesn't include the name of a function on the stack and there is no clue as to what the function is trying to do. Compare the above with:

```
delay(1000,0.5)
 .then(process1,handleError1)
 .then(process2,handleError2)
```

Also notice that as you have to pass the functions as references you don't include the parameters. If you did, i.e. if you wrote:

```
.then(process1(value),handleError1(error) )
```

then the functions would be called at once and not when the Promise was settled. The parameters are in the definition of the functions not when you pass them within a call to them.

Using named functions is arguably much easier to understand and with more appropriate function names it would be even easier. Of course the cost of this is that you have to define the functions earlier in the program, but this is worth it because it provides a more modular approach.

Using named functions makes Promises easier to understand.

Combining Promises

If you have a set of asynchronous tasks that occur one after the other then you need to chain together their Promise objects.

However, it is more common to have a set of asynchronous tasks that you want to set running, in parallel if possible, and then do something after they have all completed. In this case what you really need to do is join or combine all the Promise objects together into one Promise object that is resolved only when all of the original Promise objects are resolved.

You can combine Promises in this way using the all method. If you specify an array of Promise objects in the call to all, it returns a single "master" Promise object that is only resolved when all of the parameter Promise objects are resolved.

The onComplete of the master Promise object is passed all of the values that the parameter Promise objects return as an array.

If any of the parameter Promise objects fail and are rejected then the master Promise object fails. This means you could have some Promise objects that are still working when the master Promise object fails.

As a simple example consider two delays simulating downloading two files say:

```
var myPromise1 = delay(1000, 0);
var myPromise2 = delay(2000, 0);
myTotalPromise = Promise.all([myPromise1, myPromise2]);
myTotalPromise.then(
                function (values) {
                    console.log(values[0]);
                    console.log(values[1]);
                });
```

If you run this example you will discover that the two values returned by myPromise1 and myPromise2 are the array element that myTotalPromise prints. Keep in mind that like all Promises myTotalPromise only resolves after the UI thread is relinquished i.e. it is asynchronous.

Notice also that you may well have to keep references to the Promises that have been combined so that you can clean up after any tasks that fail. The general rule is that asynchronous processes are much harder to deal with when one fails than when they all work.

Also notice that passing an empty array results in a resolved Promise, but passing an array that doesn't contain a Promise gives different results on Chrome and Firefox.

The all function will wait until all of the Promises are resolved or at least one is rejected.

First Promise To Resolve and More!

The all function solves the problem of waiting until all of the Promises in a set resolve or at least one is rejected. You can think of this is the opposite of waiting for just one of the Promises to resolve.

There is a function that does this – race.

It will resolve when any one of the Promises resolves. The problem is that you not only get the first success, you also might well get the first rejection. This isn't usually what you want. In most cases you want to try a set of alternatives and take the first that is successful, not the first that completes successfully or rejects.

For example:

```
var myPromise1 = delay(1000, .5);
var myPromise2 = delay(1000, .5);
myTotalPromise = Promise.race([myPromise1, myPromise2]);
myTotalPromise.then(
                function (value) {
                  console.log("success");
                  console.log(value);
                },
                function(value){
                  console.log("fail");
                  console.log(value);
                });
```

In this case you see the value from the first Promise that resolves or rejects.

An even bigger problem is that usually there is no way to abort the unfinished tasks corresponding to the Promises that weren't first to resolve.

However, in most cases you need something more specific to the task in hand than the standard all or race methods. Fortunately it is very easy to implement your own Promise processing functions.

For example, what if you need the first result that is successful? In this case you have no choice but to write the logic yourself.

There are lots of other possibilities.

You could ask for a function that returns the last Promise to complete successfully so you could find out how many had worked or failed. You could ask for a function that that returned the last to fail, and so on, the combinations are many and obvious. How to combine Promises is covered in the next chapter.

Promise Error Handling

One of the big advantages of using Promises is that they make error handling easier. Not easy, but easier. Asynchronous error handling is never easy because errors can occur in a function while other functions are still executing. There is generally no way of canceling asynchronous functions, and this can make it difficult to work out what to do. However, the main problem Promises solve is detecting when something has gone wrong.

We already know that you can specify an error handler as part of the then function.

```
promise.then(processFirstFile(value), handleError1(error));
```

The handleError function will be called if the get fails for any reason i.e. if it returns an error status.

This is simple, but things get a little more complicated when we have a chain of thens. If you are running one asynchronous task after another then we have already discovered that you can do this by chaining thens.

For example:

```
var promise2=promise1.then(onSuccess1,onFailure1);
var promise3=promise2.then(onSuccess2,onFailure2);
```

where the fluent style has been avoided to show the explicit Promises returned. The first then returns promise2 that is settled when onSuccess1 returns a value or a settled Promise.

It is also helpful to keep in mind that in say:

```
var promise2=promise1.then(onSuccess1,onFailure1);
```

it is the settlement state of promise1 that determines which of onSuccess1 or onFailure1 are executed and what onSuccess1 or onFailure1 return that determines the settlement state of promise2.

However, there is an additional rule governing chained Promises. If there is no onSuccess or onFailure to handle the settlement of the Promise, then that state is passed to the next Promise and so on until there is a handler for the state.

That is, an unhandled state is passed to the next Promise in the chain.

This intentionally copies the way that exceptions work in synchronous code.

So for example if we have, writing the chain out in full for clarity:

```
var promise2=promise1.then(null,onFailure1);
var promise3=promise2.then(onSuccess2,onFailure2);
```

and promise1 is fulfilled there is no onSuccess handler defined in its then. What happens is that this state is passed to promise2 which is fulfilled and onSuccess2 is executed. Notice that the final state of promise2 would have been determined by the missing onSuccess1 handler so passing the state on is reasonable as a default.

The same rule applies to the rejection handlers. If there is no rejection handler and the Promise is rejected then that state is passed to the next handler in the chain.

Once the state has found a handler then processing resumes its normal course.

But to make sense of "normal course" we need one final rule.

Any handler that returns a value and does not throw an error passes on a success to the next Promise and this includes onFailure handlers. Any handler that throws an exception passes a reject on to the next Promise.

This all seems complicated, but the rule is that states are passed on if there is no handler for the state, and any handler that returns a value and doesn't throw an exception passes on a success to the next Promise.

For example:

```
var promise2=promise1.then(onSuccess1);
var promise3=promise2.then(onSuccess2,onFailure2);
var promise4=promise3.then(onSuccess3);
```

which would normally be written:

```
promise1.then(onSuccess1)
        .then(onSuccess2,onFailure2)
        .then(onSuccess3);
```

Suppose promise1 is rejected. As it has no onFailure handler, the rejection is passed on to promise2 which causes onFailure2 to run. Assuming onFailure2 returns a value and doesn't throw an exception, promise3 is fulfilled and onSuccess3 runs. You can think of this as a successful run of onFailure2 keeps the sequence of operations going. If this isn't what you want then throw an exception in onFailure1.

In most cases it is reasonable to leave any rejection of any Promise in a chain of Promises till the very end so aborting the chain.

For example:

```
var promise2=promise1.then(onSuccess1);
var promise3=promise2.then(onSuccess2);
var promise4=promise3.then(onSuccess3);
var promise5=promise4.then(null,onFailure4);
```

If any of the Promises are rejected then the subsequent tasks are not started and the next function to be executed is onFailure4 which is a catch all error routine.

This is such a common idiom that there is a special catch function which just sets a reject handler. So you could write the above as:

```
var promise2=promise1.then(onSuccess1);
var promise3=promise2.then(onSuccess2);
var promise4=promise3.then(onSuccess3);
var promise5=promise4.catch(onFailure4);
```

Of course even this isn't the usual way to write this because we use chaining in the fluent style:

```
promise1.then(onSuccess1)
        .then(onSuccess2)
        .then(onSuccess3)
        .catch(onFailure4);
```

which now looks a lot more like the synchronous try-catch block that it models.

To be clear, if there is a problem in any of the tasks say in onSuccess2 then effectively control jumps straight to onFailure4.

For example:

```
delay(1000, .5)
    .then(
        function (value) {
          console.log("success1");
          console.log(value);
          return delay(1000, .5);
        })
    .then(
        function (value) {
          console.log("success2");
          console.log(value);
        })
    .catch(
        function (value) {
          console.log("fail");
          console.log(value);
        });
```

In this case if either of the delay functions fail we see fail printed. So the possibilities are success1, success2 or success1,fail or just fail.

The Then Promise Chain

We are now in a position to characterize everything that there is to know about then and the Promise it returns.

The Promise then returns is initially in the pending state and is settled asynchronously.

It doesn't matter if the onComplete or the onError handler associated with the then is called, what happens to the Promise depends on the value returned.

If the handler:

- returns a value, the Promise returned by then gets resolved with the returned value as its value;

- throws an error, the Promise returned by then gets rejected with the thrown error as its value;

- returns a resolved Promise, the Promise returned by then gets resolved with that Promise's value as its value;

- returns an already rejected Promise, the Promise returned by then gets rejected with that Promise's value as its value;

- returns another pending Promise object, the resolution/rejection of the Promise returned by then will be the same as the resolution/rejection of the Promise returned by the handler;

- If there is no handler for the current state of a Promise when it resolves then that state is passed on to the next Promise in the chain that has a handler of the appropriate type.

There are lots and lots of situations in which you can use Promises that we haven't looked at. A general programming feature like Promises is capable of very varied use and a full catalog is very likely impossible. However, if you understand how they work, you should be able to work out how Promises behave in any given situation.

Summary

- Instead of accepting callbacks, asynchronous functions can and do return Promises.

- You can add the equivalent of onComplete and onError callbacks to the Promise using the then function.

- A Promise object is in one of three states. When it is first created it is pending. If the task ends correctly then it is in the resolved or fulfilled state. If the task ends with an error it enters the rejected state.

- A Promise is also said to be settled if it isn't pending. When a Promise is settled it cannot thereafter change its state.

- Handlers are called asynchronously when the Promise is settled. Any handlers that are added after the Promise is settled are also called asynchronously.

- The then function returns a new Promise which is fulfilled if its onComplete handler returns a value. If its onComplete handler returns a Promise, this Promise determines the state of the Promise returned by the then.

- Notice that in a chain of Promises the fulfillment state of a Promise determines which of the handlers it then executes and the result of the handler determines the state of the Promise that the then returned.

- If a suitable handler isn't defined for the Promise then its state is passed on to the next Promise in the chain in lieu of the state that would have been determined by the missing handler.

- If a handler doesn't throw an exception then the fulfilled state is passed on to the next Promise in the chain. That is, if the handler doesn't return a Promise then as long as it hasn't thrown an exception the next Promise is fulfilled.

- If a handler throws an exception then the next Promise in the chain is rejected.

- The catch function can be used to define an onError handler – it is equivalent to then(null,onError).

Chapter 7
Producing Promises

Promises are relatively new and this means that there are asynchronous functions that don't make use of them. This leads on to the need to promisify existing and future code. To do this you need to know a little about how Promises work internally and how to make them do what you want.

After learning how to use or consume Promises in the previous chapter the next step is to add support for Promises to asynchronous functions and to work with them to create new Promise features.

The Problem With Promises

When we first began implementing Promises there was a big problem. It was essential to provide functions so that the code that was using the Promise to signal when it was finished could change the state of the Promise, but code that was consuming the Promise using then and catch functions was unable to change the Promise's state.

That is:

only the code that created the Promise should be able to set the Promise's state.

The earliest solution to this problem of keeping the internal state private was to use a two-object solution. This is the solution that jQuery adopted in the very early days of Promises and it is a lesson in why it is not always good to be a first adopter.

A Deferred object was used by the Promise creator to manage the Promise. The Deferred had the necessary functions to resolve and reject the Promise, and the Promise had all of the functions the consumer needed, like then. In practice it was better to have the Deferred object also having all of the functions that the Promise had and so the Deferred looked like a "super" Promise object. The Deferred object was kept private to the object that created the Promise, and was used by it to call resolve and reject methods that place the Promise in the resolved or reject state.

In retrospect this is probably a mistake as it results in a confusion between what the Deferred is, and what it is used for. If you wanted to you could pass the Deferred object to the user rather than the Promise and this would allow them to change the internal state.

The two object solution to keeping the resolve and reject functions private was solved by the generalization of the mechanism long used to keep methods and properties private to an object. That is, in place of a private Deferred object which has the accept and reject methods, in the Promises standard both resolve and reject are private methods of the Promise object itself.

The Revealing Constructor Pattern

Promises use a modification on the standard way that constructors provide private methods called the revealing constructor pattern. You don't need to understand how this works to consume or even produce Promises, but it isn't difficult and it might well have other uses.

Like all JavaScript patterns once you have seen it, it seems more than obvious.

First let's see how to create a private method – if you are sure you know how, skip to the next section.

A private method is one that is created as a closure when an object is created. This is the standard method for creating a private variable accessible from within an object, but not from outside. The only difference is that the variable references a function.

For example:

```
function myConstructor(){
 var private=0;
 this.myFunction=function(){
                   alert(private);
                }
}
```

This is a constructor for an object with just one method, myFunction.

The important part is the variable called private. This is not part of the object because it isn't declared as a property of the object. so if you try:

```
var myObject=new myConstructor();
myObject.private=1;
```

you will see an error that private doesn't exist. However, as private is in scope when myFunction is declared, it is available to it as a closure. That is:

```
myObject.myFunction();
```

does display the value of private.

A private method uses the same mechanism with the small difference that the variable references a function – an inner function which is not a method of the object being constructed.

This is the mechanism that the JavaScript Promise uses to make resolve and reject private methods, but with some additional twists. The private functions and variables are accessed by a function that is passed to the constructor. Let's see how this works.

Suppose you need to set a private variable to some value, but only when the constructor is used.

The simplest solution is:

```
function myClass(value){
    var myPrivateVar=value;
    this.myMethod=function(){console.log(myPrivateVar);};
}
```

Now you can create an instance using:

```
var myObject=new myClass(10);
myObject.myMethod();
```

The value of the private variable will be printed, i.e. 10, and this has been set when the constructor was used, but the variable cannot now be altered by code external to the object.

This seems simple enough, but if we push the idea just a little further it gets a little bit more difficult. What happens if you want to pass a function in the constructor call that works with private members of the object being constructed? The function is intended to be executed by the constructor as the object is being created.

A first attempt might be something like:

```
function myClass(func) {
    var myPrivateVar = Math.random();
    var reveal = function () {
        return myPrivateVar;
    };
    func();
}
```

This creates a private variable set to a random value which can be discovered by accessing the private method reveal. The idea is that func is a function passed into the constructor and then executed which can make use of reveal to access the value.

If you try it out by passing it a function that tries to make use of reveal:

```
var myObject = new myClass(
                function () {
                    console.log(reveal());
                });
```

you will see an error message generated when func is called saying the reveal is undefined.

93

The error here is obvious, reveal is not in scope for the function passed into the constructor. Which variables a function can access is determined by where the function is declared, not where it is used. The solution to the mistake is simple enough – pass the required private members as parameters to the function.

That is:

```
var myObject = new myClass(
                function (reveal) {
                    console.log(reveal());
                });
```

Note now that the function needs to be called within the constructor with a parameter:

```
function myClass(func) {
    var myPrivateVar = Math.random();
    var reveal = function () {
        return myPrivateVar;
    };
    func(reveal);
}
```

Now it all works. The function passed to the constructor can call private functions as long as they are passed to it when the function is called.

The general principles are:

◆ Local variables and hence inner functions within an object's constructor are private to the constructor and the object it constructs.

◆ The object gains access to these private variables by closure.

◆ Private members can be accessed by the code that calls the constructor by passing parameters.

◆ If the code that calls the constructor passes a function that is executed by the constructor, this cannot access the private variables because they were not in scope when the function was defined.

◆ However, you can pass the private variables to the function as they are in scope when the constructor calls the function.

Notice that you can just as well write:

```
var myObject = new myClass(
                function (privateFunction) {
                    console.log(privateFunction());
                });
```

The name of the function is just a place holder for the first parameter passed. What the function actually is only becomes fixed when the constructor calls the function. That is when it does:

```
func(reveal);
```

This pattern is generally useful to allow external code restricted access to private functions within a constructor and of course it is how the Promise constructor allows you access to the resolve and reject functions.

The Promise Mechanism

When you create a standard Promise you use its constructor and you pass it a function, the executor, that is immediately executed by the constructor. This is the function where you create the asynchronous task and then call resolve or reject accordingly – usually when the asynchronous task has completed.

In other words this is the code that does the work.

For example, the delay function example introduced in the previous chapter can be written using JavaScript Promises as:

```
function delay(t) {
  var p = new Promise(
            function (resolve, reject) {
              setTimeout(
                function () {
                  resolve();
                }, t);
            });
  return p;
}
```

You can see that it has the same basic structure, the only difference is that now the code calls the private resolve and reject functions that are defined within the constructor. The constructor executes this immediately, passing it the private resolve and reject functions and returns the Promise.

Notice that within the function that you pass to the constructor, the calls to resolve and reject result in calling all of the onComplete and onError functions that the consumer of the Promise has set up using the then method of the returned Promise object. Only call resolve or reject when the asynchronous task has completed, and return its value or error code in resolve and reject.

Now we are in a position to understand the demonstration Promise introduced in the previous chapter:

```
function delay(t, p) {
 var promise = new Promise(
    function (resolve, reject) {
      setTimeout( function () {
                    var r = Math.random();
                    if (r > p) {
                      resolve(r);
                    } else {
                      reject(r);
                    }
                 }, t);
  });
 return promise;
}
```

You can see that what happens is we create a new Promise object which is returned to the caller almost at once. We also use setTimeout to place a function on the event queue which when its time is up calls either the resolve or the reject function with the specified probability passing the random number back as the resolved value.

The Then Parameter Problem

As delay returns a Promise, it seems obvious that it could be used in a chain (see the previous chapter). However, there is a problem.

If you try:

```
getTime();
delay(1000,0)
  .then(getTime)
   .then(delay(1000,0))
    .then(getTime);
```

where getTime is something like:

```
function getTime() {
  var time = new Date().getTime();
  console.log(time);
}
```

which shows a timer count in milliseconds, what you discover is that it appears to work, but if you look carefully the getTime functions report times that are only a few milliseconds apart, rather than 1000ms apart.

The reason should be easy to spot. The function being passed to the then function has parameters:

```
.then(delay(1000,0))
```

and this means the function is evaluated at once and not passed to the then to be activated at a later time.

The problem is that you cannot pass a parameter to a function that you use in a then.

Notice that when it is called by the Promise, the function may be passed any number of parameters depending on the way the Promise is settled.

There are a number of solutions to the problem, but none are 100% satisfactory.

The first, and most obvious, is not to use a parameter at all, but this would result in a delay function that gave a fixed time delay and this generally isn't what you want.

The second is to use a technique from functional programming called "currying" to reduce the number of parameters in the function.

For example:

```
getTime();
delay(1000)
   .then(getTime)
   .then(function(){return delay(1000,0);})
   .then(getTime);
```

In this case we have used the anonymous function to curry the delay function, i.e. we have reduced the number of parameters to zero. If you try this you will find that it works and each of the times is roughly 1000ms apart.

You can take this one-off currying and create a function that will automatically curry delay for you, for example:

```
function delay(t,p) {
  return function () {
         var promise = new Promise(
            function(resolve,reject){
              setTimeout( function () {
                  var r = Math.random();
                  if (r > p) {
                     resolve(r);
                  } else {
                     reject(r);
                  }
              }, t);
          }
        return p;
      };
}
```

You can see that this is the same idea, but now the delay function returns a function that delays for t milliseconds with no parameters. With this version of delay you can use:

```
getTime();
delay(1000)()
  .then(getTime)
   .then(delay(1000))
    .then(getTime);
```

The extra parentheses following the first use of delay are not a misprint. The delay function returns a function that delays for t milliseconds and to implement the delay it has to be called.

The need for the double pairs of parentheses is not nice, but there seems to be no way that a function that returns a Promise and accepts parameters can be used in the same way outside and inside a then.

The final way of doing the job is to use bind to curry the delay function. The bind function returns another function with a specified context and fixed values for any of its parameters. Using the original delay function we can call it in a then using:

```
getTime();
delay(1000)
  .then(getTime)
   .then( delay.bind(null,1000,0))
    .then(getTime);
```

The bind returns a function with the call context set to null and the first parameter set to 1000 and the second to 0. The call to bind is reputed to be slow.

Of the solutions, probably the best is to write the function using a parameter and remember to wrap it in an anonymous currying function if you use it in a then:

```
.then(function(){return delay(1000);})
```

This is one of the negative features of using Promises.

You have to remember that a function that returns a Promise can have parameters, but you cannot specify these parameters when you use the function in a then unless you use currying or something similar.

Composing Promises

One of the more advanced aspects of using Promises is writing functions that work with multiple Promises in various ways. Many Promise libraries provide utilities such as any, which is fulfilled if any Promise is; some, fulfilled if a fixed number of Promises are; and so on. The JavaScript Promise standard provides just two which we met in the previous chapter.

◆ all fulfilled if all are
◆ race fulfilled if one is

Rather than providing lots of different standard Promise-composing functions, it is simpler to learn how to write your own that do exactly what you want. Usually the problem is how to handle rejects, and this you can tailor to the situation.

As an example, let's implement our own simple version of the race function, race1, which also returns a Promise that resolves when the first of two Promises resolve. It is always a good idea to try to implement an idea as simply as possible and then extend it to more realistic examples.

It turns out that race1 is very easy to write:

```
function race1(p1, p2) {
    var p = new Promise(
            function (resolve, reject) {
                p1.then(
                        function (value) {
                            resolve(value);
                        },
                        function (error) {
                            reject(error);
                        }
                );
                p2.then(
                        function (value) {
                            resolve(value);
                        },
                        function (error) {
                            reject(error);
                        }

                );
        });
    return p;
}
```

All that happens is that we return a new Promise object that is resolved or rejected when any of the Promises provided as arguments resolves or rejects. To make this happen we use the then method of the two Promises to resolve or reject our new Promise.

Notice that we don't do anything to stop the other Promises from completing. It is generally difficult to cancel a pending asynchronous operation. Also notice that as a Promise is immutable, we don't need to worry about later Promises settling and trying to set the returned Promise to something different.

This can be used to get the first Promise to resolve or reject:

```
myPromise1 = delay(1000, 0);
    myPromise2 = delay(2000, 0);
    myTotalPromise = race1(myPromise1, myPromise2);
    myTotalPromise.then(
            function (value) {
                console.log("success");
                console.log(value);
            },
            function (value) {
                console.log("fail");
                console.log(value);
            });
```

In this case you will see a delay of 2000ms. Of course, you could add the race1 function as a method to the Promise object.

Extending the race function to work with any number of Promises can be done using JavaScript's iterable i.e an object that behaves like an Array.

The key is to use the map member which is supported by most browsers from IE 8 on:

```
function race1(args) {
    var p = new Promise(
            function (resolve, reject) {
                args.map(
                        function (p) {
                            p.then(
                                    function (value) {
                                        resolve(value);
                                    },
                                    function (error) {
                                        reject(error);
                                    }

                            );
                        });
            });
    return p;
}
```

You can see that all that happens is that the then method is used for each of the elements in the array. If you don't want to use map you can use a for loop instead. To make this work you have to remember to pass an array of Promises:

```
myPromise1 = delay(2000, 0);
myPromise2 = delay(1000, 0);
myTotalPromise = race1([myPromise1, myPromise2]);
```

This is an implementation of the standard race function, but it is generally held that it isn't very useful as it will return the first function to complete, even if it rejects.

What would be better is an implementation of any, which is found in some Promise libraries. Any returns the first successful result, or a reject if there is no successful function at all:

```
function any(args) {
    var number = args.length;
    var p = new Promise(
            function (resolve, reject) {
                args.map(
                        function (p) {
                            p.then(
                                    function (value) {
                                        resolve(value);
                                    },
                                    function (error) {
                                        if (--number === 0) {
                                                reject(error);
                                        }
                                    }
                            );
                        });
            });
    return p;
}
```

This works in a very similar way to race, but we now maintain a count of the number of Promises included in the arguments. Each time a Promise is rejected we reduce the count by one. If the count reaches zero then all of the Promises have been rejected and we change the state of the returned Promise to rejected. Notice that as long as one of the Promises resolves, the returned Promise resolves. As before, we make no attempt to cancel any no longer wanted Promises or tasks.

As a final example, and one that is useful in practice, let's explore a timeOut function. One of the problems with Promises is that they don't have a timeout. If a Promise isn't resolved or rejected then it will continue to be pending forever.

The following function takes a Promise and returns a new Promise that will reject if the original Promise doesn't accept or reject within the specified timeout:

```
function timeOut(p, t) {
    var promise = new Promise(
        function (resolve, reject) {
            p.then(function (value) {
                resolve(value);
            },
                function (error) {
                    reject(error);
                });
            setTimeout(function () {
                reject("timeout");
            }, t);
        });
    return promise;
}
```

Again, this is very simple. All that happens is that a new Promise is created and is resolved if the original Promise resolves, or rejected if the setTimeout is triggered first.

For example:

```
myPromise = delay(2000, 0);
timeOut(myPromise, 1000).then(
    function () {
        console.log("success");
    },
    function () {
        console.log("failure");
    });
```

In this case the Promise times out and fails. If you change the delay to less than 1000 milliseconds then the Promise succeeds. This would be easier to use as a method added to the Promise object because then it could be used with chaining.

Web Worker With Promises

So far we have only considered the problem of adding Promises to asynchronous functions which run on the UI thread. However, Promises are also useful when working with other threads. It is obvious as that a Worker thread doesn't share objects with the UI or any other thread, the Promise has to live in the UI thread and be resolved or rejected by what the Worker thread does. What this means is that we have to wrap the creation and use of the Worker thread in a function that runs on the UI thread and returns a Promise.

As an example we can add a Promise to our Worker thread example that computes Pi in the background.

We need to package the interaction between the UI thread and the Worker as a function:

```
function piWorker() {
    var worker = new Worker("pi.js");
    var promise = new Promise(
            function (resolve, reject) {
                worker.addEventListener("message",
                                    function (event) {
                                        resolve(event.data);
                                    });
            });
    return promise;
}
```

This first sets the Worker thread off and then creates a Promise which has a function which resolves the Promise when a message is received from the Worker thread.

So how do we use the new function and the Promise object it returns?

The answer is, as before, that you use it just like any other asynchronous function that returns a Promise.

```
button1.addEventListener("click",
        function (event) {
            button1.setAttribute("disabled", true);
            piWorker().then(
                    function (value) {
                        result.innerHTML = value.pi;
                        count.innerHTML = value.k;
                        button1.setAttribute("disabled", false);
                    });
        });
```

The button's event handler now just has a simple call to the piWorker function and this immediately returns a Promise object. The then method of the Promise object is used to define what should happen when the thread completes and returns the "Promised" value. That is the function passed to then sets the button caption to the value and re-enables the button.

This is very much easier to use as the fact that we are using a separate thread is completely hidden from the client. In addition, the client is able to define what is to be done with the result without having to delve into the inner workings of the function.

Thenables

JavaScript isn't a typed language and all that is needed for something to have the essential properties of a Promise is that it has a then method that accepts an onComplete and onError function and returns a value or a Promise. You can convert anything that has a then method, a thenable, into a full Promise using the constructor's resolve method:

```
var promise=Promise.resolve(thenable)
```

You can also pass the method a value or another Promise. In the case of the value the returned Promise is resolved at once, but keep in mind that this occurs asynchronously. If you pass it a Promise then the return Promise is settled when the supplied Promise is and reflects its state and value. A call could pass a thenable – an object with a method called then that accepts at least two parameters and returns a value or a Promise. If the call passes a thenable then the return Promise is linked to the then in the sense that it is settled when it gets a value, or the Promise is settled.

You can use the resolve method to convert non-standard Promises into something that is more standard. For example, you can use it to convert a jQuery Promise into a standard Promise:

```
var promise=Promise.resolve(jQueryPromise);
```

As well as resolve the constructor also supports the reject method which returns a Promise in the rejected state.

Reporting Progress

In previous versions of the Pi program running on a Worker thread we added a periodic update. Many asynchronous tasks are better implemented if they keep the user informed of progress often using the update to control a progress bar as part of the UI.

So how do we report progress when the asynchronous operation returns a Promise?

Some implementations of the Promise object add a third optional function to the then method:

```
promise.then(onComplete,onError,onProgress);
```

For example the Promise object provided by jQuery does just this. However, JavaScript standard Promises don't incorporate this option. The reason is that an onProgress function would compromise the purity of a Promise as an object with a simple state transition from pending to settled. However, in the real world we still need a way to provide feedback to the user.

We have to use Promises with progress reporting.

There are several ways of doing this, but the most direct is to modify the then function of the returned Promise to support an onProgress function. To do this we have to subclass the supplied Promise constructor and this is fairly tricky because of the way Promises make use of the revealing constructor pattern.

First we have to modify the Worker thread code so that it returns a status object which indicates that it is providing an update rather than signalling that the asynchronous operation is complete:

```
var state = {};
state.phase="running";
state.k = 0;
state.pi = 0;
var i;
var time=Date.now();
for (i = 0; i < 100000000; i++) {
    if(Date.now()-time>1000){
        this.postMessage(state);
        time=Date.now();
    }
    state.k++;
    state.pi += 4 * Math.pow(-1, state.k + 1) / (2 * state.k - 1);
}
state.phase="complete";
this.postMessage(state);
```

Now after every second the postMessage method is used to pass the state back to the UI thread. A new property, phase, is used to indicate whether the message is an update or a final value:

running means this is an update

and

complete means that the Promise should be resolved.

This is a general principle. If the Worker thread is going to support updates as well as a final value it has to send an indication of the type of the postMessage event – update or final.

Now we have to modify the piWorker function so that it returns a Promise with a then method that supports onProgress. To do this we have to replace the then method that is native to the Promise object with our own. This is essentially overriding a method, but on an object rather than a class as is common in other languages.

For example to override the then method of Promise all we have to do is:

```
var superthen = promise.then.bind(promise);
promise.then = function (onComplete, onError, onProgress) {
    progress = onProgress || progress;
    return superthen(onComplete, onError);
};
```

The first line is the most important. It saves a reference to the then method with this bound to the Promise object. Next we set the then method to a new function which has three parameters not two, and pass the first two parameters to the old version of the then method. The third we simply store in a local variable created at the same time as the Promise. Notice that we have to call the superthen method and return its value to make sure that chaining still works. The then method has to return a Promise.

If we assume that the then method is overridden we can concentrate on implementing the piWorker function to accommodate the progress function:

```
function piWorker() {
    var worker = new Worker("pi.js");
    var progress = function () {};
    var promise = new Promise(
            function (resolve, reject) {
                worker.addEventListener("message",
                        function (event) {
                            if (event.data.phase === "running") {
                                progress(event.data);
                            } else {
                                resolve(event.data);
                            }
                        });
            });
...
```

The function starts off in the usual way by starting the worker thread off. It then creates the progress variable and initializes it to an empty function – this way we don't have to add a special case to deal with what happens if the user doesn't provide a custom progress function. The Promise is created in the usual way, but now the message event handler has to test the phase of the thread – running or complete. If it is running then progress is called, if not then the Promise is resolved.

The complete piWorker function is:

```
function piWorker() {
    var worker = new Worker("pi.js");
    var progress = function () {};
    var promise = new Promise(
            function (resolve, reject) {
                worker.addEventListener("message",
                    function (event) {
                        if (event.data.phase === "running") {
                            progress(event.data);
                        } else {
                            resolve(event.data);
                        }
                    });
            });
    var superthen = promise.then.bind(promise);
    promise.then = function (onComplete, onError, onProgress) {
        progress = onProgress || progress;
        return superthen(onComplete, onError);
    };
    return promise;
}
```

Using piWorker is now only slightly more complicated in that we have to supply an onProgress function:

```
button1.addEventListener("click",
        function (event) {
            button1.setAttribute("disabled", true);
            piWorker().then(
                    function (value) {
                            result.innerHTML = value.pi;
                            count.innerHTML = value.k;
                            button1.setAttribute("disabled", false);
                     },
                    function () {},
                    function (value) {
                            result.innerHTML = value.pi;
                            count.innerHTML = value.k;
                    });
        });
```

This approach works, but if you are going to use a lot of Promises with an onProgress function then it is a good idea to create a new type Promise type complete with constructor.

The ProgressPromise Object

A more general solution is to subclass the Promise to create a new Promise object which includes an onProgress feature. Most of the details are as before, but there are some interesting problems in reusing an object that makes use of the revealed constructor pattern.

The constructor starts off simply enough. We need a private variable to store a reference to the new progress callback:

```
function ProgressPromise(action) {
    var progress = function () {};
```

The action function passed to the constructor now takes the form:

```
var promise=new ProgressPromise(
                function(accept,reject,progress){...});
```

The progress function is up to us to write code to handle, but the part of the function that involves accept and reject can be handled by the original Promise object.

To do this first we need to recast the action function into the usual accept and reject form:

```
var action2 = function (resolve, reject) {
                action(resolve, reject, progress);
            };
```

To understand this idea just consider what happens when a Promise is constructed using this new action2:

```
var promise = new Promise(action2);
```

The Promise will call action2 with resolve and reject set to the correct functions. Action2 then calls action with resolve and reject set correctly and our extra progress function. This should be enough for action to complete its tasks and make use of resolve, reject and progress.

Finally all we have to do is override then to make use of the three functions rather than just two:

```
    var superthen = promise.then.bind(promise);
        promise.then = function (onComplete, onError, onProgress) {
        progress.onprogress = onProgress||progress.onprogress;
        return superthen(onComplete, onError);
    };
    return promise;
}
```

If you put all this together we can try it out using:

```
function piWorker() {
    var worker = new Worker("pi.js");
    var promise = new ProgressPromise(
            function (resolve, reject, progress) {
                worker.addEventListener("message",
                    function (event) {
                        if (event.data.phase === "running") {
                            progress(event.data);
                        } else {
                            resolve(event.data);
                        }
                    });
            });
    return promise;
}
```

Notice now that we are using ProgressPromise and using the three functions specified in the constructor.

If you try this out you will discover that it doesn't work.

The reason is subtle. It is all due to the way the progress variable is captured in the closure. The problem is that there are two closures involved. The first is the closure captured by the Promise created in the ProgressPromise constructor. The second is the closure created so that the function in addEventListener can access the parameters resolve, reject and progress. This means that the event handler and the then function each have their own captured copy of the progress variable and when the then modifies its copy the event handler still has the original empty function.

This problem of more than one closure not sharing a single copy of a variable occurs occasionally and the solution is to make both copies reference a single object and make the changes to that object. Both captured variables will be referencing the same object and so both closures will reflect changes to that object.

In the case of the ProgressPromise it makes more sense to make use of a function object rather than a general object. The reason is that the Promise should provide general functions which implement the resolve, reject and progress options rather than just calling one function that the user has supplied. For example if you want to handle multiple possible onprogress functions you would have to create a queue of them and then progress would have to call each one in turn.

In this case we can keep it simple by only allowing a single onprogress function:

```
function ProgressPromise(action) {
    var progress = function (value) {
        progress.onprogress(value);
    };
    progress.onprogress = function () {};
    var action2 = function (resolve, reject) {
        action(resolve, reject, progress);
    };
    var promise = new Promise(action2);
    var superthen = promise.then.bind(promise);
    promise.then = function (onComplete, onError, onProgress) {
        progress.onprogress = onProgress||progress.onprogress;
        return superthen(onComplete, onError);
    };
    return promise;
}
```

This looks complicated, but now progress is a function which calls the onprogress function stored as a property. Notice that the then has to be changed to store the onprogress function correctly.

Now everything works.

You can use the same techniques to extend the Promise object to have other methods and properties. For example, you could add an indicator of how long the Promise had lived, a state indicator and a cancel method. All of these take you away from the Promise standard and it is important not to underestimate the challenge in getting a new Promise facility right.

Notice that ProgressPromise is more appropriately called a thenable rather than a Promise.

Beyond Promises

Once you understand the way Promises can be used to trigger other Promises the only problem is that you will go too far with the idea. Keep it simple and only write the code you actually need. Promises are a reasonably good solution to the asynchronous problem, but the soon to be common async and await is so much better. However, as we will discover in the next chapter, even async and await are based on Promises, and a good understanding of Promises is important to mastering async and await in more challenging situations.

Summary

- Promises are designed to restrict access to the resolve and reject functions to the code that creates the Promise.

- This used to be done using a separate deferred object which was kept private.

- The Promise standard makes use of the revealing constructor pattern to keep resolve and reject private, while allowing the code that creates the Promise to submit to the constructor a function that makes use of them.

- The revealing constructor pattern extends the way a closure provides private variables and functions to the constructed object by passing private variables to a function that is passed to the constructor.

- The functions that are called by the resolve and reject functions are set by the then method. As with callbacks you cannot pass parameters to these functions because this causes them to be evaluated.

- The basic Promise object provides two ways to combine Promises – all and race – but it isn't difficult to create new functions which combine Promises in any way that you need. For example you can create a Promise with a timeout or a version of race that returns the first Promise to resolve, not just the first to settle.

- You can arrange to return a Promise when you start a new worker thread and use this to obtain the final result of the thread.

- One problem with using Promises with Worker threads is that they provide no way to handle an update message for progress reporting.

- It is possible to modify the then function of a Promise so that it can be used to specify an onProgress handler.

- It is also possible, but not straightforward, to derive a new Promise object from the standard one, which implements the then that makes use of an onProgress handler.

Chapter 8

The Dispatch Queue

Now that we have met the Promise we have all that we need to examine the dispatch queue in more detail. Many of the ideas in this chapter have been introduced earlier, but now is a good time to explain the deeper ideas and some alternatives.

Tasks and Microtasks

Our earlier description of the event or dispatch queue is slightly over-simplified. Now that we have explored many of the possible ways of working with the queue it is time to find out some finer points of how it works.

It is clear that each thread of execution gets its own queue. All of the windows from a single origin share the same queue, and this is used by the postMessage method to allow them to communicate.

Tasks are originally the only thing placed in the event queue, but modern JavaScript and browsers also now support microtasks. The event loop takes tasks one at a time and allows the task to run to completion before the next task is serviced. Tasks can also be preferentially dequeued according to their source. This allows the system to prioritize some tasks.

A subtle, but sometimes important point is that the browser may render updates to the page between servicing tasks. This is important because if your code makes changes to the page you will generally only see these changes if you allow the UI thread to service the queue and there has to be a task waiting for it to perform the update.

Microtasks were introduced partly as a lightweight version of the task, but more to introduce a new class of task that was guaranteed to be executed before the next task starts i.e. as soon as possible.

That is the microtask queue is processed after each task has completed.

Any microtasks that are created while the microtask queue is being processed are added to the queue and processed before moving on to the next task. Also no page updates are performed until the next task is processed. This means that microtasks aren't slowed down by page rendering.

The big problem with this task/microtask split is that browsers aren't consistent in the way that they implement it. The reason is that ECMAScript describes things in a different way to HTML 5. ECMAScript has jobs which are the same thing as microtasks. At the moment the only way to find out with certainty if something is placed in the task or the microtask queue is to write a program to test what order things happen in.

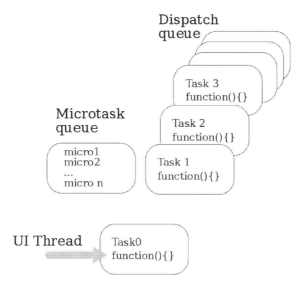

The important points are:

- ◆ Tasks are taken from the queue and run to completion.
- ◆ Microtasks are processed when the current task ends and the microtask queue is emptied before the next task is started.
- ◆ Any microtasks created while the microtask queue is being processed are processed before the next task.
- ◆ The browser may render updates between tasks.
- ◆ The browser does not render updates between microtasks.

The sequence is:

`task ends→all microtasks are processed → page updates → next task`

Notice that if the UI thread is freed and there are no tasks to process, the microtask queue is still cleared.

In general older features, events and methods like setTimeout work by adding tasks to the queue. Newer features that need to be processed rapidly like Promise settling add microtasks to the queue. At the moment the only things that use microtasks in browser-based JavaScript are the Mutation observer and the Promise. The Promise object adds a microtask to the queue for each of its callbacks. It is also worth keeping in mind that not all browsers support microtasks.

In most cases you can ignore the distinction between task and microtask, but just occasionally you will encounter some unexpected behavior which doesn't make sense unless you know about microtasks.

Adding a Microtask

One of the recurring problems in JavaScript is finding a way to add something to the dispatch queue. For reasons that are difficult to work out there is resistance to adding commands that directly interact with the queue and this leaves JavaScript programmers with the responsibility of inventing ways to do the job with the commands they have. For example for tasks the most obvious way is to use setTimeout, although this isn't a very good solution.

For microtasks there is a more direct way, but it relies on the JavaScript engine implementing Promises correctly as microtasks – most do, but with slight variations in implementation. To add a microtask to the queue all you have to do is:

```
Promise.resolve().then(function(){...)});
```

The Promise.resolve method returns a resolved Promise object and its then method can be used to add a function to the microtask queue. Recall that even for a resolved Promise its callbacks are executed asynchronously.

We can try this out and demonstrate the way that microtasks behave with a simple program:

```
setTimeout(function () {
    console.log("Task1");
}, 0);
Promise.resolve().then(function () {
    console.log("MicroTask1");
});
setTimeout(function () {
    console.log("Task2");
}, 0);
Promise.resolve().then(function () {
    console.log("MicroTask2");
});
```

This uses setTimeout to add two tasks and Promise.resolve to add two microtasks. The order that they are added in suggests that we should see:

```
Task1
MicroTask1
Task2
MicroTask2
```

but on the current version of Chrome, Edge and Firefox what we see is:

```
MicroTask1
MicroTask2
Task1
Task2
```

You can add as many microtasks and tasks as you like and you will see all of the microtasks executed before the tasks. You might be wondering why Task1 was printed first. The reason is that the microtask queue is emptied first when the code that sets the tasks/microtasks ends.

In principle microtasks are always processed first.

You can use this program as a test to see if an object is queuing a task or a microtask. Simply replace the Promise.resolve by whatever you want to test.

Promises Are Not Fully Async

You may have noticed that there is a small problem with microtasks hidden in the description that the microtask queue is emptied before the next task and any microtasks that are generated while it is being processed are added to the queue and executed.

The general assumption is that Promises are asynchronous and this in turn implies that they are non-blocking and executing any number of short Promise callbacks cannot block the UI thread because it is serviced between each one.

This isn't true.

No tasks are processed while the microtask queue is being emptied.

For example:

```
setTimeout(function () {
        console.log("Task");
    }, 0);

var p=Promise.resolve();
for(i = 0; i<100; i++)
   p.then(function () {
        console.log("MicroTask");
    });
```

If you run this you will see "MicroTask" 100 times and then "Task". The 100 items on the microtask queue blocks the servicing of the task queue until it is emptied. This effectively freezes the UI for the duration. If you would like to see what happens simply increase number of repeats to 10,000 and you will discover that the UI freezes for that time. Although it isn't part of the standard, some browsers have implemented a maximum number of microtasks that will be serviced in one go. This does free the UI every now and again, but you will still find it difficult to do anything.

Obviously generating 10,000 thens isn't a very good idea and this sort of problem is unlikely to actually occur in practice. If it does you need to rethink the way you are doing the job. The problem is that there are other ways that the same thing can occur – chained Promises and combined Promises using all, say, can all add multiple microtasks to the queue that keep the UI thread busy without an opportunity to service tasks. It is important to know that breaking up a process into multiple microtasks does not keep the UI responsive.

Node.js setImmediate & nextTick

Node.js has two useful functions which can create tasks and microtasks.

The setImmediate function will queue a task just like setTimeout, but without any timing restrictions. It has been implemented in Edge and IE 10 and later, but it has been removed from Chrome, Firefox and Safari.

For example:

```
setImmediate(function () {
              console.log("Set Task");
          });
```

adds the function to the task queue and it will be executed as fast as possible, but after any microtasks.

Where it is supported it is faster than postMessage, but it is only safe to use in Node.js.

As well as a task queue, Node.js has a microtask queue that is used for the same things as in a modern browser. In addition it has the process.nextTick function which can be used to queue a microtask:

```
process.nextTick(function () {
              console.log("Set Microtask");
          });
```

In the case of node.js you can also use the process.maxTickDepth to set the number of consecutive microtasks that will be processed before a task is.

There is no support for nextTick in any browser, but:

```
Promise.resolve().then(function(){...);});
```

does the same job.

Adding a Task

We have already looked at ways of adding tasks to the queue as it is far too basic an async programming technique to be left until later. The big problem is that JavaScript doesn't have a standard way of doing the job directly.

The only one that works on nearly all browsers is setTimeout. This works, but as pointed out before it is slow. The HTML5 specification limits the time delay to a minimum of 4ms. This is enforced by most browsers and this means that your custom event is going to a little slower than you might expect from a zero millisecond delay. Some older browsers make use of an even longer minimum delay of 10ms. Of course the timeout will not happen until the function that used setTimeout finishes and hands back the UI thread to the dispatcher. This means that typically you can arrange for around 200 tasks per second.

If speed isn't an issue then SetTimeout is the best way to add a task to the queue:

```
setTimeout(function () {...}, 0);
```

If speed is important then the usual solution is to use postMessage to the same window:

```
window.addEventListener("message",function(){...});
postMessage("fire", '*');
```

This is capable of 20,000 tasks per second i.e. 100 times faster than setTimeout. The only problem is that it isn't supported well enough on any version of IE and this can be a problem in some cases.

The two methods of adding tasks to the queue listed above are the best known, but there are many others. You can use any event that you can fire in a truly asynchronous way to add a task to the queue. Of course the problem is that as explained in Chapter Two dispatchEvent does not run the event asynchronously and so it isn't of any use in this case.

You will also encounter the advice that using a resolved Promise to add a task is good and fast. It is fast, but as we have found it adds a microtask and not a task to the queue. If this doesn't matter then by all means use a Promise, but once again notice that there is no support on legacy browsers and no version of IE supports Promises.

There are many ingenious methods of adding tasks to the queue. In particular, there are many variations on using postMessage to send a message from an iFrame, another window, a worker, and so on. These work, but they are not as fast as sending a message to the same window.

One of the most ingenious approaches uses the HTMLImageElement to generate an error event:

```
var image = new Image();
image.addEventListener("error", function () { … });
image.src = 'data:,xxx';
```

There clearly is no image resource called xxx and so the error event fires. This works and the Image object is supported by nearly all browsers. It is faster than setTimeout at around 10,000 tasks per second, but not as fast as postMessage.

You can probably find alternatives ways of adding a task to the queue. All you need is a way to trigger a true asynchronous event, typically some error event on an object that you can construct using code. The difficult part is finding something that works fast.

RequestAnimationFrame

The is one final function that allows you to hook into what the task queue is doing. The requestAnimationFrame method will add a task that is run just before the dispatcher updates the page, i.e. just before it renders. This is obviously the best way to run any code that you need to modify the page.

To add a function to the queue use:

```
window.requestAnimationFrame(function(){...});
```

The function is passed a timestamp which gives the current time in milliseconds when the callbacks start to be executed. All callbacks receive the same time. Also notice that this is not a repeating event and you have to add the function to the queue again to ensure that it is triggered on each page update.

The event is triggered typically 60 times per second, but it is determined by the refresh rate of the display. It can be less if the system is trying to save power in background mode. There is no point in updating the display any faster than this because it simply will not be displayed.

Notice that requestAnimationFrame is slower than setTimeout in nearly all situations and it is supported in all modern browsers, but only in IE 10 and later.

Summary

- The dispatch queue is slightly more complex in a modern browser and supports two types of entry – task and microtask.

- Tasks correspond to the classical entity placed on the event queue – click events, timer events and so on.

- Microtasks were invented to allow a quicker response for some types of event.

- The microtask queue is maintained separately from the task queue, and before the next task is taken from the queue all of the microtasks are serviced and the microtask queue is emptied.

- Page updates only occur between tasks.

- You can use Promise.resolve().then(function(){...}); to add a microtask to the queue.

- Because all microtasks are processed before the next task, Promises and microtasks in general are not fully async.

- It is possible to put so many microtasks in the queue that the UI becomes unresponsive. To stop this JavaScript engines limit the number of microtasks that can be serviced at once.

- Node.js provides the setImmediate function to add a task to the queue without any delay. This is not supported by browsers.

- Node.js also provides process.nextTick to add a microtask to the queue.

- There is no standard JavaScript way of adding a task to the queue and setTimeout which is often used is slow and can only add 200 tasks per second. PostMessage is often 100 times faster, but isn't supported on legacy browsers. There are other methods, but none are as quick as postMessage. An alternative method is to use an Image Object.

- RequestAnimationFrame can be used to queue a task that is called just before the browser renders the page. This is triggered at the display's frame refresh rate which is usually 60 times per second.

JavaScript was and is an asynchronous language in the sense that it was invented in an event-driven environment and mostly used in an asynchronous environment. Yet until recently the language wasn't well suited to asynchronous programming and was only armed with the callback and the closure. Today the latest version of JavaScript not only has the Promise, it also has the async and await commands which together with the Promise make asynchronous programming easy.

If you are a novice to intermediate programmer then you can simply use async and await as if they were magic designed to solve all of your problems. Indeed one danger is that innocent programmers might grow so comfortable with asynchronous programming that they might forget that is what it is.

While async and await make asynchronous programming easy and less error-prone, if you are going to use it in creative or indeed in any way but the most basic, a thorough understanding what is going on is very important.

Async Pretends To Be Sync

With the Promise we almost have everything we need to make asynchronous code really easy to use. Indeed we have almost enough to make it look exactly like synchronous code.

For example, suppose you have a long running function that operates asynchronously and returns a Promise, then at the movement you might use it something like:

```
var promise=slowFunction();
promise.then(onComplete,onError);
```

The then method provides the code that is to be run after the Promise is settled.

This good, but how much easier it would be if we could write:

```
var promise=slowFunction();
wait for slowFunction
continue with program
```

This would keep the natural order of the code. Of course you can't just wait. This is a beginners mistake to think that the code can simply loop until the slowFunction completes. This doesn't work because JavaScript is single-threaded and while the code was waiting no events would be processed and the UI would freeze.

However, suppose the wait could be implemented so that it freed the UI thread and allowed it to process any events, only returning to the code when the slowFunction had completed. This would allow us to write the code as if it was synchronous and still keep the UI serviced.

This sounds easy, but for it to be useful the wait would have to ensure that the state was saved when the UI thread was doing something else, and was restored when the code restarted. For example if a for loop was in progress then the state of the for loop would have to be preserved and restarted after the wait.

What is interesting is that we already have a command that can save the state and resume code – the yield instruction. As already described, see Chapter 4, yield was introduced to allow generators to be implemented. However, it can also be used to save the current state. In the early days yield was, and still is, used to implement facilities that are now provided by async and await. You could basically do something like:

```
var promise=slowFunction();
yield;
continue with program
```

Of course you would have to arrange that the yield freed the UI thread and that the slow Function restarted the code again. This is the basis of the polyfills used to provide async and await in environments that don't support it.

Lets now see how async and await work.

Basic Async

There are two parts to async and await, and while they work together it is important to understand what each one does.

Let's start with async.

If you apply the async keyword to a function, it is converted into an AsyncFunction object with the same code.

An AsyncFunction object is a special type of function that can be suspended to wait for an async operation using the await command.

Put more simply: you can only use await within a function that is marked as async.

Notice that you don't have to use await within an AsyncFunction, but there isn't much point in creating one if you don't.

For example:

```
var myFunc= async function {
  return 1+2;
};
```

converts the function into an AsyncFunction object stored in myFunc with the same code.

An AsyncFunction object has the same code, but with one big difference – it returns a Promise. The Promise is created automatically when the function starts executing. The Promise is returned with whatever the original function returned as its resolved value. If the function returns a Promise then the new Promise simply reflects its state. If the function doesn't return a value then the Promise has a resolved value of undefined.

So if you try:

```
console.log( myFunc());
```

you will see not 3, but [object Promise].

If you need the resolved value of the Promise you have to use its then method:

```
myFunc().then(
               function(value){
                   console.log(value);
               });
```

So this is the first rule of async/await:

♦   every async function returns a Promise.

It is also true that, for a range of reasons, you can't use async in the top level code because it always has to be applied to a function.

In practice you don't have to use a function expression to create an async function, a standard function declaration will do.

For example:

```
async myFunc function {
  return 1+2;
};
```

works in exactly the same way.

You can also use async to convert a value into a Promise that wraps that value. For example:

```
var p=async function(){return v;}();
```

converts v into p, a Promise which resolves to it. Notice the final parentheses - this is an immediately-invoked function expression (IIFE).

Basic Await

The second rule of async/await is:

- ◆ you can only use await with an AsyncFunction i.e. with a function that has the async keyword prepended.

This is simply because only an AsyncFunction has the necessary extras to allow it to be suspended and resumed.

The await operator can be applied to any Promise and this pauses the function's execution until the Promise is fulfilled. That is, it really does await the Promise's fulfillment.

- ◆ If the Promise is resolved the await operator extracts the resolved value and returns it.
- ◆ If the Promise is rejected then the await throws an exception with the rejected value.

Thus await converts a Promise into a result or an exception just as if it was a result from a synchronous function.

If you use await on a value that isn't a Promise, it simply returns that value at once without pausing the function's execution.

You should now be able to see how it all fits together.

Within an AsyncFunction you can write code as it if was synchronous by waiting for each Promise to resolve.

For example:

```
async function myFunction(){
    var first=await delay(1000,0);
    var second=await delay(2000,0);
    return first+second;
};
```

This first waits for one second and then for two seconds. Notice that the Promise returned by the delay is "unwrapped" and the random value is stored in first and then second. Also notice that as an async function, myFunction returns a Promise so to call it from the top level you would have to use:

```
myFunction().then(function(value){console.log(value);});
```

This is the basic idea of using async and await, but there are some subtle points we need to consider if we are really going to master what is going on.

The main issue is what does the thread do while the async function is awaiting and when exactly does the function resume?

Where Does The Thread Go?

Now we come to the most subtle point about the way that async and await work in JavaScript – and this makes it different from what might happen in other languages.

The question is, what does the thread do while a function is paused because of an await?

There are many ways of answering this and ways of thinking about it, but the best is to imagine that the await behaves like a return that can be resumed. When a function executes an await, the thread returns to the calling program which receives the Promise object created by the async function in a pending state. It really is as if a return had been executed, the only difference is that the function can resume when the Promise it is waiting for is settled.

If you find this behavior odd it is worth pointing out that it is also the way that the yield command works. A yield lets the thread resume from the point that the function was called just like a return, but again with the option of restarting.

For example consider the example:

```
async function myFunction(){
   var first=await delay(1000,0);
   var second=await delay(2000,0);
   return first+second;
};
```

What happens when myFunction is called is that the first await causes a Promise to be returned which resolves after three seconds to the value of first+second.

You can think of this as being equivalent to:

```
function myFunction(){
   return new Promise(function(resolve,reject) {
                      var first=await delay(1000,0);
                      var second=await delay(2000,0);
                      resolve(first+second);
                   };
```

This behavior has some consequences that are worth pointing out.

The first is that you can only write code that looks synchronous within an async function. At the top level you still have to work with Promises.

The second is that it is difficult, but not impossible, to use await to allow the UI thread to service the event queue. The problem is that when you use the await command the UI thread continues to run the code that called the function, and the UI thread is only freed when this terminates.

There is also the small matter that the async function cannot resume while the thread is busy running other code. In other words, the thread has to be freed and goes back to servicing the event queue in order for the async function to be resumed, or put another way the async function is resumed asynchronously.

This has a strange consequence. The first await in an async function lets the calling program continue, but the function will only resume if the calling function has terminated. This means that that any second or subsequent await in an async function will only be executed after the calling program has terminated.

Some simple examples will help make these ideas clearer.

Consider a simple pause function:

```
async function pause(t) {
    console.log("before");
    var promise = new Promise(
            function (resolve, reject) {
                setTimeout(
                        function () {
                            resolve();
                        }, t);
            });
    await promise;
    console.log("after");
}
```

You can see the general idea is to await a Promise that takes t milliseconds to resolve. There are two console.log commands that serve to give the time before and after the await.

If you try it out from the main program:

```
pause(1000);
```

you will see the before and after messages separated by about a second. However, if you try it out using;

```
console.log("Before call");
pause(1000);
console.log("After call");
```

You will see:

```
Before call
before
After call
```

followed a second later by:

```
after
```

This should make sense if you have followed the idea that the await returns the Promise in a pending state. What happens is that "Before call" and

126

"before" are displayed without delay, but then instead of waiting for one second the await returns control to the main program which immediately prints "After call" and then frees the UI thread. One second later the Promise resolves and the function resumes to print "after". Not the order of events you were hoping for.

If you change the program to:

```
console.log("Before call");
pause(1000).then(function () {
    console.log("After call");
})
```

then you will see the one second delay and the messages "Before call/before" followed one second later by "after/After call".

Also notice that the await cannot be resumed until the main program has completed and this mean if it is long running then the delay could be much longer than one second.

Async & Await Summary

- ◆ The async operator changes a function into an AsyncFunction object which has the same code, but returns a Promise.

- ◆ The Promise is returned to the calling function in a resolved state when the async function returns a value or a resolved Promise of its own.

- ◆ The Promise is returned to the calling function in a rejected state if the async function throws an exception or returns a rejected Promise of its own.

- ◆ The Promise is returned to the calling function in a pending state if the async function performs an await.

- ◆ An await which can only be used in an async function acts like a return that can be resumed.

- ◆ You can await any Promise object and the await returns a Promise of its own that is linked to the Promise object – i.e. pending if the Promise object is pending and so on.

- ◆ When the awaited Promise object is settled, the async function is resumed at the next instruction. The Promise object is unwrapped to its resolved value or an exception is thrown.

- ◆ As there is no way of marking top level code as async, you cannot use await in top level code, only in an async function.

If you understand the simplicity of the way that async and await work then how to use them should be obvious, but it is worth making sure that everything is clear and it is worth looking at some potential problems.

Flow of Control

The huge advantage of using async and await is that, at last, asynchronous code doesn't distort the flow of control.

For example, if you want to include an async function within a loop, you just do:

```
async function myFunction() {
    var i;
    for (i = 0; i < 10; i++) {
        var r = await delay(1000, 0);
        console.log("r="+r+" i= "+i);
    }
}
```

In this example, delay is the function introduced in Chapter 6:

```
function delay(t, p) {
 var promise = new Promise(
   function (resolve, reject) {
     setTimeout( function () {
                    var r = Math.random();
                    if (r > p) {
                       resolve(r);
                    } else {
                       reject(r);
                    }
                }, t);
  });
 return promise;
}
```

In this case you will see the value of r printed, one every second, and the value of i steps from 0 to 9. Compare this with how you would achieve the same result using a raw Promise.

The same simplicity applies to other type of loops and to conditionals.

For example:

```
 async function myFunction() {
    if(await delay(1000, 0)<0.5){
       console.log("Less than 0.5");
    } else {
       console.log("Greater than or equal to 0.5");
    }
}
```

You can use an async function anywhere you can use a standard function, and this includes within a condition or an expression.

For example:

```
async function myFunction() {
   return 1+await delay(1000, 0)*10;
}
```

In this case the expression is completed after one second and the value of the Promise is used.

Error Handling

Just as async and await don't distort the flow of control when things are working, neither does it distort the flow of control when things go wrong. As the await converts the reject status of the Promise to an exception you can continue to use try-catch.

For example:

```
async function myFunction() {
   try{
      var r = await delay(1000, 0.5);
   }catch(v){
      console.log("error "+v);
      var r=0;
   }
   return r;
}
```

You can, of course include multiple lines in the try clause. If you don't wrap an async function in a try-catch and an error occurs then a Promise is returned in the rejected state.

This means you can write:

```
var r=await delay(1000,0.5).catch(v){console.log("error "+v);};
```

In most cases it is better to use try-catch, but at the top level, of course, you can't use await and hence normal Promise handling applies.

If you don't use try-catch or the catch method then a Promise error is thrown.

Parallel awaits

If you are just introduced to the await instruction as a way to call an async function, then you can get some of the goodness out of the idea and it is well worth knowing about and using, but if you know about Promises and the way async and await work with then, then you can do a lot more. For example, you can easily arrange for multiple asynchronous functions to run at the same time, and you can await them individually. The trick is to simply use the functions to get the Promises and then await them at a later time.

For example:

```
async function myFunction() {
    var p1 = delay(1000, 0);
    var p2 = delay(1000, 0);
    var r = await p1;
    console.log(r);
    r = await p2;
    console.log(r);
    return r;
}
```

In this case we get two Promises from the one second delays and then await them one after the other. The two delays run at more or less the same time and so the total delay is about one second not two. The awaits also unwrap the Promise values in the usual way and hence we can display the value of r. The only subtle point is to notice that it matters what order you await the settling of the Promises. In this case the first await waits for p1 and nothing more happens until it is settled – the state of p2 is irrelevant.

Await Combined Promises

Once you have seen this sort of use of await, inventing more complicated uses is fairly obvious. For example, you can use the Promise combining methods to create a single Promise to await.

For example, using the race method you can await the first Promise to complete:

```
async function myFunction() {
    var p1 = delay(1000, 0);
    var p2 = delay(1000, 0);
    var p = Promise.race([p1, p2]);
    var r = await p;
    console.log(r);
    return r;
}
```

As explained earlier, the only problem is that race returns a Promise that is settled by whichever Promise settles first, irrespective of whether it is resolved or rejected. You can, of course, use the techniques introduced in Chapter 7 to combine Promises, and so determine what you are awaiting.

The Top Level Problem & Async Event Handlers

The way that async and await have been integrated with Promises is very clever, but there is a problem with the way you cannot make use of them in the top level code i.e. the "main" program. The way that an await allows the thread to return to what it was doing before a function is called is logical, but it stops you doing various things. For example, you cannot write a pause function that can be used to pause the top level code – it simply returns a

Promise at once. There is also the fact that an async function cannot resume until the thread is freed and able to service the event queue.

At first all of this seems like a big problem that spoils the way async and await make asynchronous code easy to use. In practice it isn't such a big problem because no well designed JavaScript program should have a long running main program. As explained in Chapter 2, the main program is simply a way of getting things set up and it should complete quickly. From this point on the program is essentially a set of event handlers waiting to be executed.

The good news is that you can define an async event handler and this means that as much of the code in the core of your program can be async code as you care to define. Once the top level program has completed the way things work is much simplified because in an event handler an await always frees the thread to process its event queue.

For example, consider the task of making a button flash by changing its background color. This is the sort of task where the beginner often makes the mistake of writing something like:

```
button2.addEventListener("click",
      function (event) {
         while (true) {
            button2.style.backgroundColor = "red";
            for(i=0;i<10000;i++){}
            button2.style.backgroundColor = "white";
            await pause(1000);
            for(i=0;i<10000;i++){}
         }
      });
```

By this point in your study of asynchronous code and the single-threaded JavaScript environment you should have no trouble with why this doesn't work. The while loop never releases the UI thread and so the whole UI freezes. However, changing the function to an async function which awaits on a pause function makes everything work:

```
button2.addEventListener("click",
      async function (event) {
         while (true) {
            button2.style.backgroundColor = "red";
            await pause(1000);
            button2.style.backgroundColor = "white";
            await pause(1000);
         }
      });
```

It works because an await in an event handler is like a resumable return and so it frees the UI thread to process the event queue – which includes returning to the function when the await receives a fulfilled Promise from the pause function:

```
function pause(t) {
    var promise = new Promise(
            function (resolve, reject) {
                setTimeout(
                        function () {
                            resolve();
                        }, t);
            });
    return promise;
}
```

Notice that the pause function isn't an async function – it doesn't need to be as it doesn't use await. However, some might want to include async as a way of indicating that it returns a Promise.

It is true that async functions tend to form a nested set as each layer waits for the Promise returned by earlier layers. However, it is important to remember that a function doesn't have to be an async function for you await it – it just has to return a Promise.

DoEvents – Microtasks

One very early attempt at taming asynchronous code is the doEvents command in Visual Basic. This simply yielded the UI thread and allowed the event queue to be processed. When all of the events had been processed the thread returned to the instruction after the doEvents command. This provided a very simply way for a long running function to keep the UI active.

The doEvents command came into some disrepute because of a lack of reentrancy control. An event handler could use a doEvents command only to be restarted because it has to handle another event in the queue. Of course there were ways to control this reentrancy problem, but overall doEvents was discouraged in favor of using tasks with separate threads.

The await command looks as if it might be a way to implement a doEvents command. It is, but there are some interesting problems in getting it to work and these reveal some of the more subtle details of how events are handled in modern JavaScript.

A simple minded doEvent function could simply return a resolved Promise that another function could await:

```
function doEvents() {
    return Promise.resolve();
}
```

Of course, as the Promise is resolved there is nothing to await, but it still causes the thread to be released to process the event queues.

So, for example, we could use doEvents to keep the UI active while using a loop to compute Pi:

```
button2.addEventListener("click",
    async function computePi() {
        var pi = 0;
        var k;
        for (k = 1; k <= 10000000; k++) {
            pi += 4 * Math.pow(-1, k + 1) / (2 * k - 1);
                if (Math.trunc(k / 1000) * 1000 === k) {
                    result.innerHTML = pi;
                    count.innerHTML = k;
                    await doEvents();
                }
        }
    }
);
```

If you try this out you will find that it doesn't work. Sometimes you will see a partial update, but most often you will only see the final result after the function has finished running.

The reason that this doesn't work is that, as described in the previous chapter, Promises make use of the microtask queue which is separate from the main task queue. Microtasks have a priority over tasks in the sense that the microtask queue is emptied after a task completes. What this means is that all Promises resolve and run their then method before the next full event is started. This is sometimes important to know, but the really important difference between the microtask queue and the task queue is that between tasks the browser may render the UI. What this means is that it is only when the full task queue is serviced does the UI have even a chance to render.

The solution to our non-working doEvents function is to make sure it causes the task queue to be processed. The simplest way to do this is to add an event to the queue using setTimeout. If you change doEvents:

```
function doEvents() {
    return pause(0);
}
```

where pause is the function given in the previous section that uses setTimeout, then you find it works and the UI is updated and remains responsive throughout the computation.

When you release the UI thread with an await, the event queue is only processed if there is an event waiting in the queue that relates to the returned Promise, and the UI is only updated when the event queue is processed. What this means is that you cannot simply return a resolved Promise and rely on the fact that Promises are always resolved asynchronously – in this case only the microtask queue is processed.

The only way to force the task queue to be processed with a Promise is to create a task that is needed to resolve the Promise.

For example you can use:

```
function doEvents() {
    var promise = new Promise(
               function (resolve, reject) {
                   requestAnimationFrame(function () {
                   resolve();
               });
           });
    return promise;
}
```

and this waits for the next animation frame before doing the update which is what we want.

Reentrancy

A big problem of approaches like doEvents and hence to async and wait is that they provide no obvious protection against the reentrancy problem. Reentrancy is what it sounds like – it is when a thread enters a section of code that another thread is already executing. In a single-threaded environment this can only happen if you have an instruction such as await or doEvents which pauses the code and provides the opportunity to start it once again. In this case the same thread starts to execute the code it hasn't finished.

In most cases code is not written to be reentrant and the result is usually some unexpected behavior if not a system crash.

The question is, what happens in JavaScript if a function is reentered?

The answer is surprisingly simple – functions are largely reentrant in JavaScript.

For example, consider the program in the previous section that computes Pi using doEvents to keep the UI responsive. Suppose the user clicks the button more than once. To make it easier to see what is going on change the doEvent function to read:

```
function doEvents() {
    return pause(5000);
}
```

This makes it easier to see what is going on by inserting a longer pause. You might think that the result would be a mess as the for loop that is suspended by the await is restarted by the user clicking the button a second time. In fact the for loop isn't restarted. Every function evocation in JavaScript starts the execution of the function off from the start, but each resume after the await restores all of the variables back to their original values. As this can only happen if the UI thread has been freed by the new invocation being paused by an await, the two invocations take turns running.

This largely makes JavaScript reentrancy safe, but not completely so.

Consider this version of computePi:

```
state = {};
state.k = 0;
state.pi = 0;
async function computePi() {
    state.pi = 0;
    for (state.k = 1; state.k <= 10000000; state.k++) {
     state.pi += 4 * Math.pow(-1, state.k + 1) / (2 * state.k - 1);
          if (Math.trunc(state.k / 1000) * 1000 === state.k) {
              result.innerHTML = state.pi;
              count.innerHTML = state.k;
              await doEvents();
          }

    }
}
```

The only change is that now the result is being stored in a global state object. If you try the same experiment what you will find is that now clicking the button a second time resets the computation back to zero.

What is happening is that the global state object is being shared between all of the invocations of the computePi function. When a new invocations starts it zeros the properties of the state object and when the old invocation resumes it uses the same, newly zeroed, state object. Sharing global objects isn't a good idea unless you have some special behavior in mind.

If we change state to be a local variable:

```
async function computePi() {
    var state = {};
    state.k = 0;
    state.pi = 0;
```

Then we return to the previous case where the object that state references is restored when the thread resumes after the await with the effect each time the user clicks the button another independent computation starts running.

Worker Threads

There is nothing unique about the UI thread when it comes to async and await. You can define async functions in a Worker thread and await them in the usual way. Notice that in this case the event queue that is involved doesn't have any events from the UI and this is a simplification.

You can use the doEvents approach to periodically free up the Worker thread so that it can respond to any messages sent to it from another thread.

For example we can implement the thread control pattern from Chapter 5 using doEvents:

```
async function computePiAsync() {
    var k;
    for (k = 1; k <= 1000000; k++) {
        pi += 4 * Math.pow(-1, k + 1) / (2 * k - 1);
        if (Math.trunc(k / 1000) * 1000 === k)
            await doEvents();
    }
}

function doEvents() {
    return pause(0);
}
async function pause(t) {
    var promise = new Promise(
            function (resolve, reject) {
                setTimeout(
                        function () {
                            resolve();
                        }, t);
            });
    return promise;
}
```

Notice that this is essentially the program given earlier, but now we use await doEvents in computePiAsync to free the Worker thread. The message event handler is unchanged:

```
var pi=0;
this.addEventListener("message", function (event) {
    switch (event.data) {
        case "start":
            computePiAsync();
            break;
        case "update":
            postMessage(pi);
            break;
        case "stop":
            close();
            break;
    }
});
```

To make use of the worker we need:

```
var worker = new Worker("pi.js");
worker.addEventListener("message",
            function (event) {
                    result.innerHTML = event.data;
            }
);
worker.postMessage("start");
setInterval(function () {
            worker.postMessage("update");
        }, 100);
```

Notice that without the doEvents the update message would only be handled at the end of the computation.

You need to include some code to stop the function being started again before it has finished and all of the considerations with reentrant code apply to Worker threads.

Summary

- Async and await appear to make asynchronous code look like synchronous code.

- Marking a function as async makes it return a Promise at once and its returns are converted into calls to resolve with the returned value.

- You can await the resolution of any Promise including one returned by an async function. Awaiting a Promise is like performing a return that can be resumed.

- When an async function performs an await the thread returns to the calling function. It is only when the thread is freed that the await can resume.

- When the Promise resolves, await unpacks the value returned. If the Promise is rejected the await throws an exception. This allows you to await an asynchronous function as if it was a synchronous function.

- Using await you can place asynchronous functions within loops and conditionals as if they were synchronous functions.

- If you know how async and await work you can implement other ways of dealing with results. For example you can run asynchronous functions in parallel or await their combined state.

- You can use async and await to implement a doEvents function which releases the UI thread to service the task queue. However, because this is based on using a Promise, you have to be careful to allow the UI thread to service the task queue so that the UI is updated.

- JavaScript functions that do not use global objects are largely reentrant.

- You can use async and await within Worker threads.

Chapter 10

Fetch, Cache and ServiceWorker

There are a number of new features in JavaScript that make good use of Promises and hence async and await.

The Fetch API is a replacement for the XMLHttpRequest function and perhaps the jQuery Ajax function. It also has a big role to play in the action of a ServiceWorker. If you are using modern JavaScript you probably should be using Fetch.

The Cache API is also of use in a ServiceWorker, but it is also generally available to JavaScript code. You can use it to store and retrieve resources and it is largely a replacement for the soon-to-be-removed appCache.

Finally we come to the ServiceWorker, which is a modified form of the WebWorker designed to provide a life for your app when connectivity isn't available, but it is so much more than this. It intercepts all of the traffic from the rest of your app and can completely control what is returned. In this sense it not only provides a way to allow your app to work when offline, it also provides opportunities for modifying how the app updates when it is online.

Fetch, Cache and ServiceWorker are three key components in a new approach to web apps – the progressive web app or PWA. There are a number of libraries that make use of ServiceWorker, perhaps most notably Angular CLI, but you don't have to adopt a library or framework to get the advantage of using ServiceWorker.

Basic Fetch

The Fetch API is a modern implementation of the XMLHttpRequest and it can be used to download almost any file the browser has access to and to send data to the server using Get or Post.

The basic idea is really simple. All you have to do is use the fetch function:

```
fetch("URL");
```

This performs a Get request for the URL specified and returns a Promise that eventually resolves to a response object. The fetch function is available in the Window and WorkerGlobal contexts.

Most HTTP errors are also returned as a resolved Promise and a response object that specifies the error. The reject state is reserved for communications errors.

You could use the Promise's then method to specify what happens to the response, but it is much simpler to use async and await:

```
async function getText(){
    var response=await fetch('myFile.txt');
```

For a simple file get this is almost all there is to using fetch. The response object returned has a set of methods and properties that allow you to discover the status of the request and retrieve the data.

For example, the status property returns the HTTP status code – usually 200. As already mentioned HTTP errors such as 404 no such page are returned as resolved Promises and you have to handle them as errors. You only get a rejected Promise if there is something wrong that is more reasonably characterized as an exception. You can also retrieve the headers sent from the server using the headers property which returns a Headers object.

Notice that at this stage we only have the HTTP headers and status, the data are still to be fetched across the network.

The Response.body gives you access to a readable stream. This allows you to read the data in a chunk at a time. This is useful when, for example, you are trying to work with something that is too big to fit in memory or when data is being continuously generated. The Streams API is another new feature that makes use of Promises. To read the Response in chunks you would use something like:

```
var reader=Response.body.getReader();
```

and following this each time you use the read method a Promise which resolves to the next chunk of the stream is returned:

```
var data=await reader.read();
```

The data is of the form

```
{value:chunk,done:boolean}
```

where value is the data and done is true if this is the last chunk of data.

Notice that a stream can only be read once unless it is recreated.

Streams are very low level compared to what most people want to do with retrieved resources. For this reason the Body object also implements a set of higher level stream readers. These return a Promise that resolves after the entire stream has been read to the data in a processed format.

Currently the supplied formatted readers are:

```
arrayBuffer
blob
formData
json
```

and

```
text
```

and each returns a Promise which resolves to the type of data you have selected.

One subtle point is that you can only retrieve a response's data once. This is obvious if you keep in mind that the methods that retrieve the data are stream readers – you can only read a stream to the end once. However, it can cause problems if you mistake these methods as simply providing format conversion.

For example:

```
async function getText(){
    var response=await fetch('myFile.txt');
    console.log(response.status);
    console.log(await response.text());
}
```

This retrieves the data in the file as text. Once the response body has been retrieved or "used" you cannot repeat the operation.

That is:

```
async function getText(){
    var response=await fetch('myFile.txt');
    console.log(response.status);
    console.log(await response.text());
    console.log(await response.text());
}
```

Throws an exception:

```
Uncaught (in promise) TypeError: Already read
```

You can check to see if the body has been used via the bodyUsed property of either the request or the response. If you do want to access the data in more than one format then you have to make use of the clone method – see later.

Request Object

Things are only a little more complicated when you want to do something more than just a get. You can specify a second parameter, the init object, in the call which controls the type of request made.

The init object has lots of properties, but the most important are:

- method – the request method e.g. GET, POST, PUT etc
- headers – a header object
- body – the body of the request which is sent to the server.

You can find the full specification in the documentation.

If you want to repeatedly fetch the same resource it is better to create a Request object which has all of the properties of the init object plus a URL property. You can pass the Request object to fetch in place of the URL parameter and it acts as the init object as well.

So the previous fetch could be implemented as:

```
async function getText(){
    var request=new Request('myFile.txt',
                 {
                     method:'GET'
                 });
    var response=await fetch(request);
```

Notice that you can reuse a request object even if you have streamed the body data of its associated Response. However, as already commented you cannot reuse a Response object after you have read its body data.

You can also obtain a duplicate Request or Response object using the clone method. This can be useful if you aren't sure that the response will be valid. For example, to first check to see if the response if valid json we could use:

```
var response = await fetch(request);
var res2 = response.clone();
try{
     console.log(await res2.json());
   } catch (e) {
     console.log(await response.text());
   }
```

If the response isn't valid json it is displayed as text. Notice you have to clone the response before trying to retrieve the body. You cannot clone a stream that has been read.

You can use a fluent style to make this look neater:

```
var response = await fetch(request);
try{
     console.log(await response.clone().json());
   }
catch (e) {
     console.log(await response.text());
   }
```

The clone method introduces a buffer into the equation and the data is streamed into a local buffer from where it can be accessed a second time. This has the side effect of keeping the data in memory until all of the copies are read or disposed of.

FormData, Get & Post

The most common fetch operations that go beyond a simple get are get with a query string and posting form data.

Let's see how to do both of these tasks.

The data that we want to send could come from anywhere, but a traditional form element is simple and common:

```
<form id="myForm" >
   First name:<br>
   <input type="text" name="first" value="Enter Data">
   <br>
   Last name:<br>
   <input type="text" name="last" value="Enter Data">
   <br>
   <br>
   <input type="submit" value="Submit">
</form>
```

Now all we need is to handle the submit event:

```
myForm.addEventListener('submit',
     function (event) {
        event.preventDefault();
        sendData();
     });
```

The sendData function does the actual work using fetch, but first we need to construct a query string that can be added to the URL. It is strange that JavaScript has had no standard way of doing this until recently and at the moment not all browsers support the new features.

If you don't want to use the new FormData and URL APIs then your best option is either to do the job directly, use a polyfill or use jQuery:

```
async function sendData() {
    var url = new URL("http://url/myFile.php");
    var formdata = new FormData(myForm);
    for (var p of formdata) {
        url.searchParams.append(p[0], p[1]);
    }
    var request = new Request(url, {
        method: "GET"
        });
    console.log(url.toString());
    var response = await fetch(request);
```

The FormData object creates a set of key/value pairs from the form with the keys being the ids and the values being whatever the user entered. This is then converted to a query string using the searchParams method of the URL object. Finally we build a request object specifying a GET and perform the fetch.

The url is something like

```
http://url/myFile.php?first=Mickey&last=Mouse
```

assuming that the user entered Mickey Mouse as the first and last name. This is sent to the server which will process it and do whatever is appropriate with the data before returning a response which we can either collect using a command like:

```
await response.text();
```

or we can opt to ignore it.

Sending form data using a POST is even easier as we can send a FormData object without having to convert it.

```
async function sendData() {
    var url = new URL("http://url/myFile.php");
    var formdata = new FormData(myForm);
    var request = new Request(url, {
        method: "POST",
        body: formdata
        });
    var response = await fetch(request);
```

The formdata will be unpacked into the body and sent to the server. A Content header is also set automatically so that the server can check the format of the data.

Notice that as a Request object has a body you can access it using the same methods as in a Response object. As for the Response object, once you have used the body data you can't use it a second time. You can of course clone it if you really want to treat it as different formats.

This is about all there is to know about the new APIs. There are still things to learn and implement, but these problems are not any different from using other methods of transferring data. Currently the facilities offered by fetch aren't as extensive as what you will find in say jQuery, but it has to be taken into account that fetch is the way of the future.

There are also some new features in the Fetch API that help with the problem of canceling and controlling a request, but these aren't standardized as yet. In addition it is worth knowing that you can access the lower level data streams used to access the body data. This offers the possibility of creating very sophisticated processing.

Cache

The cache API is a replacement for appCache and it is much more flexible. Its basic operation is very simple. The CacheStorage object stores a set of Cache objects each of which stores a set of key value pairs.

The key is a request object and the value is a response object.

That is, a Cache object stores request/value pairs and the CacheStorage object stores Cache objects.

The idea is that you can segment your cache storage scheme into different Cache objects which you can then use via the CacheStorage object. In the simplest situation you can just use a single Cache object for everything you want to store, but even here you have to think about the possibility of supporting versioning with multiple Cache objects.

The CacheStorage object keeps an index by name of the Cache objects you create. You can use its open method to create and/or retrieve a Cache object by name, and the match method will search all of the Cache objects for the first occurrence of the request object and return its associated response object. Notice that if there are multiple Cache objects storing the same request/response pair, the one you get is the one that was created first. If you want more control you should use open to retrieve the particular Cache object and then use its match method to retrieve the request/response pair from it.

The final part of the puzzle is that the global CacheStorage object is called caches. So to create a new Cache object you would write:

```
var myCache=await caches.open("myCache");
```

If the cache already exists it is just opened ready for use.

All of the Cache methods are asynchronous and return Promise objects or arrays of Promise objects.

To store a new key/value pair in the cache you would use either:

```
await myCache.add(request);
```

which loads the response from request and stores both or:

```
await myCache.put(request,response);
```

which stores the request and response pair in the cache without fetching anything new.

There is also addAll which will add an array of requests and their response objects freshly download.

There is a complication here.

When you use add or addAll the response is downloaded and the body is also downloaded and stored in the cache in a raw form. When you use put the response isn't downloaded again, but the body has to be stored in the cache in raw form. If you have used any of the commands that set the body data to a particular type then it will not be stored in the cache and you will generate an exception.

Another way to say this is that the body cannot be used before it is put into the cache. You also cannot use the body of a response after it has been put into the cache. To use it you have to retrieve it from the cache.

For example if you try:

```
var response = await fetch(request);
await myCache.put(request,response);
```

you will find that it works and the request/response pair are stored in the cache. However, you cannot use the response body after this. That is if you now try:

```
var text=await response.text();
```

you will see and error that says:

```
Uncaught (in promise) TypeError: Already read
```

You can only read the body data in once and adding a response to the cache reads it and you cannot read it a second time. In the same way if you use the body before putting the response in the cache you will see the same error.

When you store a response in the cache its body is streamed and stored and cannot be streamed a second time.

To find something already stored in the cache you can use:

```
await myCache.match(request,options);
```

which returns the first response objects in the cache or:

```
await myCache.matchAll(request,options)
```

which returns an array of Promises with all of the response objects that match the request.

So to save something in the cache and retrieve it you would use something like:

```
var response = await fetch(request);
var myCache = await caches.open("myCache");
await myCache.put(request, response);
var response2 = await myCache.match(request);
var text = await response2.text();
```

Alternatively you could simply use add to both fetch and store the response:

```
var myCache = await caches.open("myCache");
await myCache.add(request);
var response = await myCache.match(request);
var text = await response.text();
```

It is important to realize that you can store multiple responses to the same request. The search options also allow you to control the nature of the match. For example setting ignoreSearch to true ignores any query string in the URL.

It is also worth mentioning that at the moment there is some disagreement when the Promises will settle. Some browsers wait for the response to finish downloading, others don't.

You can mange the cache using:

```
await myCache.delete(request);
```

which returns true if the request is found and deleted.

The keys method returns an array of keys that the request matches. If you don't specify a request all of the keys are returned. A prime use of this is to delete all of the entries in a Cache object:

```
var keys=await myCache.keys();
for(req of keys){
    myCache.delete(req);
}
```

Notice that as we don't await each of the deletes they occur in parallel.

If you want to delete an entire Cache object then use the CacheStorage object's delete method:

```
caches.delete(cacheName);
```

If want to delete all of the Cache objects you can use the CacheStorage object's keys method in a very similar way to deleting the entries in a Cache object.

```
var keys=await caches.keys();
for(cache of keys){
    caches.delete(cache);
}
```

You can also use the CacheStorage object's match method to find a response irrespective of which Cache object it is stored in, and its has method to discover if a particular Cache object exists.

One interesting problem is finding out how much storage is available. You can do this using the storage API. This provides the estimator object which has two properties, quota and usage. So to find out how much you have used and how much is available:

```
var estimate = await navigator.storage.estimate();
console.log(estimate.usage);
console.log(estimate.quota);
```

Under Chrome the quota was: 65,941,658,828 bytes. The big problem is that this is an estimate and the documentation says that there might be more, but you can't rely on it.

This is about all there is to say about the CacheStorage API, but there is the always problematic issue of security. CacheStorage will only work on HTTPS connections. Browsers that support CacheStorage generally provide an option to relax this constraint for testing purposes. It is also that case the HTTP from localhost is allowed.

A Cache Example

Putting all of this together it is time for a very simple example. Let's retrieve an image file, store it in a Cache object and then retrieve it from the Cache. The HTML is simply:

```
<body>
    <img id="image1"/>
    <img id="image2"/>
</body>
```

The code is just as simple, but as we want to use async and await it is all packaged into a function that can be called from the main program:

```
<script>
getImage();

async function getImage() {
```

Getting the image is simple, we need a request object and then we can retrieve it and display it:

```
var url = new URL("http://localhost/MainLogo.png");
var request = new Request(url, {
                    method: "GET"
                });
var response = await fetch(request);
var blob = await response.blob();
var objectURL = URL.createObjectURL(blob);
image1.src = objectURL;
```

After this the image appears in image1. Next we store it in the cache using add:

```
var myCache=await caches.open("myCache");
await myCache.add(request);
```

Notice that this downloads the response again.

Now we have created the Cache object and stored the request/response pair in it. Next we can retrieve the response from the Cache:

```
        var response2=await myCache.match(request);
        var blob2 = await response2.blob();
        var objectURL2 = URL.createObjectURL(blob2);
        image2.src=objectURL2;
    }
</script>
```

If you use the browser to inspect the network traffic you should be able easily confirm that the file is downloaded just twice, once by the fetch and once when it is added to the cache and blob2 is retrieved from disk cache.

The Service Worker

The fetch and cache API are general and can be used by the UI thread or by a Worker thread, but they are both very much connected with the new Service Worker. This promises to make HTML-based applications behave much more like desktop applications. It is, some think, the solution for which we have been looking for a long time.

What is so special about the Service Worker?

The first is that it has a life all of its own separate from the web page that it is associated with. Service Workers are downloaded, installed and activated. From then on the Service Worker is downloaded at least every 24 hours. Any page that the user opens that is within the Service Worker's scope results in it being run – even if the page doesn't reference it. This is very strange behavior for a JavaScript program. It behaves more like a browser add-on than a script in a web page.

The second is that a Service Worker intercepts all resource requests from the pages it is associated with – those that are within its scope. That is, if the page requests a resource via a particular URL the Service Worker intercepts this request and can either supply its own response or it can allow the resource to be downloaded by the browser in the usual way. Typically the Service Worker might use a Cache object to try to retrieve the resource and only fall back to the network if it is unavailable or if a fresher version is desirable. This approach is often referred to as "offline first" as it allows the app to operate even when the network isn't available, however, there are many other use cases.

Notice that after the Service Worker has been installed it is invoked every time the browser fetches a resource that is associated with the Service Worker. The Service Worker doesn't have to be re-installed or reloaded from the original page. Once installed the browser manages it and activates it as needed. In fact one of the problems you first encounter is how to stop a Service Worker once you have started it. In general management of Service Workers is one of the more difficult aspects of using them.

As for the Cache API, Service Workers are restricted to HTTPS for security reasons. You can test your code using a localhost-based HTTP server in Chrome and Firefox.

Registering Service Workers

A Service Worker is just a special type of Web Worker and it runs in its own global context with its own thread and has no access to the DOM. You can use the postMessage method to trigger message events in the UI thread, and so on. The first difference is that you have to register a Service Worker using the register method. You have to supply the name of the file containing the code and an option object which currently supplies the scope of the URLs that are going to be associated with the Service Worker.

The default scope is the location of the Service Worker and all subfolders. The optional scope can only narrow the range of URLs that that the Service Worker will handle. Also notice that any resource requested by a page within the scope of a Service Worker is also passed to the Service Worker.

Another subtle point is that the Service Worker is only registered after the page that is registering it has finished loading. From this point on, however, it intercepts all URLs in its scope including the one for the page that loaded it if this is in the scope. What this means is that a Service Worker cannot modify the resources being loaded by the page that registers it as it is loading.

So, for example, to register a Service Worker to manage traffic to all of the URLs in the site you would use:

```
async function reg() {
 await navigator.serviceWorker.register("\myWorker.js");
}
```

That is, the Service Worker is stored in the root of the site and so all of the site's URLs are within its scope.

If myWorker.js contained:

```
console.log("loaded");
```

then you would see loaded displayed in the console when the reg function is called. Of course in practice you would have to check that serviceWorker was supported and handle any registration errors, but all this is omitted in the examples for clarity.

150

The register method returns a ServiceWorkerRegistration object which has a range of useful status indicating properties:

◆ scope – the scope

and three state indicators:

◆ installing

◆ waiting

and

◆ active.

Notice that you don't have to check to see if a Service Worker is already registered. You can use the register method as often as you like and the browser will keep track of the latest version registered.

After a successful registration the Service Worker is available for use – it is active. Every time a page within its scope is loaded it is run. The browser also downloads the file if it is online and checks to see if the code has changed. If the code has changed by even a single byte the new version of the Service Worker is installed. However, it then enters the waiting state until the current Service Worker has finished being used. This means that all of the pages that are in scope have to be closed. When a page that is in scope is next opened the Service Worker enters the active state and starts to process requests.

There are also events associated with the state changes which we will look at later. It is also possible for a waiting Service Worker to force a takeover of the pages that are being processed by the older version.

What all this means is that once a Service Worker has been registered to a browser it becomes a permanent part of the web site defined by its scope. The Service Worker persists across browser and machine restarts. There is no need to register the Service Worker more than once, but if you do it does no harm.

Fetch Event

Once your Service Worker is registered and active it runs its own event queue and you can write event handlers that will be called as necessary.

The key Service Worker event is fetch which is generated whenever a page requests a resource which is within the Service Worker's scope or by a request from a page within that scope.

For example, if we add to the Service Worker:

```
addEventListener("fetch",function(event){
    console.log(event.request.url);
});
```

and place a button on the page that registers the Service Worker with the event handler:

```
button1.addEventListener("click",
                    async function (event) {
                      var response = await fetch('myFile.txt');
                      console.log(await response.text());
                    });
```

Now if the page is loaded and the button clicked you will see the request url in the console followed by the text stored in the file. If the fetch event handler simply returns then the browser's default fetch is used. In other words, any resources in the scope of the Service Worker that it doesn't want to modify are handled in the usual way.

If it does want to interfere in the resource then the respondWith method of the FetchEvent object can be used to return a custom response. Usually the custom responses are automatically generated either by being accessed via a Cache object or being downloaded from a different request. It is possible, however, to construct responses from scratch and it is worth seeing how to do it. First we need a suitable response object:

```
var init = {"status": 200, "statusText": "Generated"};
var myResponse = new Response("myText", init);
```

The Response constructor takes the body as the first parameter and in this case it is simple Unicode text.

Once we have the Response object it can be sent back to the requesting thread using respondWith which accepts a Promise as its only parameter:

```
event.respondWith(
        new Promise(
                  function (resolve, reject) {
                      resolve(myResponse);
                  }));
```

If you want to avoid the explicit use of a Promise you can use the idiom introduced in Chapter 8:

```
event.respondWith(async function(){return myResponse;}());
```

The async modifier converts the function into an AsyncFunction which wraps its return value in a Promise.

In fact the simplest thing to do is pass a Response object which will be treated as if it was a Promise by respondWith:

```
event.respondWith(myResponse);
```

If you try this out within the fetch event handler you will find that the second time the page is loaded it is replaced by "myText" as this is now the response for all URLs in the Service Worker's scope.

To make things a little more easy to follow we need to restrict the URLs that the custom response is returned for:

```
addEventListener("fetch", function (event) {
    console.log(event.request.url);
    if (!event.request.url.includes("myFile.txt"))
        return;
    var init = {"status": 200, "statusText": "Generated"};
    var myResponse = new Response("myText", init);
    event.respondWith(myResponse);

});
```

Notice that now the URL is tested and the custom Response is only returned if it contains "myFile.txt". Now if you click the button you will see the "myText" in the console rather than the contents of the file.

There is a subtle point that you need to keep in mind when using respondWith. If the fetch event handler doesn't call respondWith, the browser will fetch the resource in the usual way. However, if the event handler awaits for some function to complete i.e. is asynchronous before calling respondWith, the thread is freed and the browser decides that the event handler isn't going to call respondWith and so fetches the resource.

What this means is that if you are going to handle the fetch you need to call respondWith before you release the thread with an await.

The simplest way to deal with this problem is to always supply an async function to respondWith that deals with the fetch. That is:

```
addEventListener("fetch", function (event) {
        event.respondWith(doFetch(event));

});
```

where doFetch is an async function that contains whatever code is needed to complete the fetch.

Setting Up The Cache – waitUntil

Now you can begin to see how powerful the idea of the Service Worker is. In many ways it is the "real" entity of the app that you are creating as it persists even when the user isn't browsing your website. In most cases what you want the Service Worker to do is to cache resources and retrieve them when pages within the scope request them. As you already know how the Cache object works, this is fairly easy apart from the problem of initializing the cache.

153

This is where the status events come into the story.

There are two status events:

◆ Install - fires when the Service Worker is ready to be initialized.

◆ Activate – fires when the Service Worker takes over from any earlier versions and is ready to do work. This is where you can clean up anything from previous versions.

Notice that the state events are triggered when the Service Worker's state changes:

Installing → Install event → Waiting → Activate event → Active.

It is also important to be clear that these events only fire once when the Service Working is being registered or when it is being updated. That is, they only occur once for each version of the Service Worker.

So to set up a Cache object all we need to do is create an Install handler:

```
addEventListener("install", async function (event) {
    console.log("install");
    var url = new URL("http://localhost/myFile.txt");
    var request = new Request(url, {
        method: "GET"
    });
    var myCache = await caches.open("myCache");
    await myCache.add(request);
});
```

This handler creates and loads myCache with myFile.txt when the Service Worker is installed.

There is a small problem with this event handler that might well go undetected for some time. Consider for a moment what would happen if the Cache loading involved a great many and perhaps large files – not just one small file as in this test case. There is no problem with keeping the thread too busy, however, as we are using asynchronous functions and awaiting them. While the files are being downloaded the thread is free.

The problem is that when we await a Cache add in the event handler we free the thread and it continues where it left off. In this case it is installing the Service Worker and when we await in the event handler it continues to install the Service Worker. The problem is that it might well finish installing the Service Worker before the Cache has been completely loaded.

To avoid this sort of problem we have the new extendableEvent and its waitUntil method. This tells the event dispatcher that when it gets the thread back it is not to complete the task in hand. Instead it is to wait until the Promise provided resolves. If the Promise resolves then the Service Worker is installed. If it rejects then the entire installation fails. This stops incomplete Service Workers from being used.

To protect our Cache loading we need to include all of the asynchronous function calls within waitUntil. For example:

```
addEventListener("install",
        function (event) {
            console.log("install");
            var url = new URL("http://localhost/myFile.txt");
            var request = new Request(url, {
                method: "GET"
            });
            event.waitUntil(
                    async function () {
                        var myCache = await caches.open("myCache");
                        var response = await caches.match(request);
                        if (response === undefined)
                            await myCache.add(request);
                    }());
        });
```

Notice that we pass waitUntil an async function that performs all of the Cache loading and execute it immediately. Given that waitUntil needs to be passed a Promise that resolves when the initialization is finished, you might be worried that we don't actually return a Promise or even a value. We don't need to because the Promise constructed by the async modifier resolves to undefined when the function completes.

The need to "hold" an event while releasing the thread is something that occurs in other parts of Service Worker and you can expect to see extendableEvents occurring in other places.

Finally, there is another subtle point to keep in mind about the lifetime of the cache. The cache persists beyond the life of a Service Worker version. What this means is that in this case the install event occurs when a new version of the Service Worker is being prepared and the event handler retrieves myCache and loads a new version of myFile.txt into it.

New Service Worker versions should either work with the existing Cache or they should create new versions of the Cache and delete the old one once they are active. It isn't a good idea to delete or modify the Cache in the install event handler because any active previous version will still be using it. It is better to wait for the new Service Worker to become active and then delete or modify the original Cache.

For example, if you want the Service Worker to create and load the Cache only when it is registered for the first time you would use something like:

```
addEventListener("install",
        async function (event) {
            console.log("install");
            var url = new URL("http://localhost/myFile.txt");
            var request = new Request(url, {
                method: "GET"
            });
            var myCache = await caches.open("myCache");
            var response = await caches.match(request);
            if (response === undefined) {
                await myCache.add(request);
            }
        });
```

Notice that all we do is check to see if the entry is in the cache and only load it if it is.

Fetch

With the Cache object set up and loaded we can now define a fetch event handler:

```
async function doResponse(event) {
    var response = await caches.match(event.request);
    if (response === undefined)
                return fetch(event.request);
    return response;
};
```

This function can be called within the fetch event handler:

```
addEventListener("fetch",
        function (event) {
          console.log(event.request.url);
          event.respondWith(doResponse(event));
          });
```

The reason for using a function in this way is because using an await within the event handler would free the thread and if this occurs before respondWith the browser will assume that you don't want to handle the fetch. Any asynchronous work has to be done in the respondWith call. You can, of course, use an IIFE in place of a named function.

The fetch event has a waitUntil method, that is it is an extendableEvent, however, you usually don't need to use this explicitly as respondWith automatically uses it to extend the event until the response is available.

Controlling The Service Worker

When you start to do more complicated things with Service Workers what you will find is that keeping track of which version is actually running is difficult. The fact that your new version will not be installed until all of the pages that are using the old version have been closed is one problem. A more subtle problem is that the new version will not be activated until the page that causes it to be installed has finished loading. This means you usually need a refresh of that page as well as navigating to another page first.

You can modify the way a new version of a Service Worker takes control. The ServiceWorkerGlobalScope method skipWaiting forces the Service Worker to take control i.e. to become active, without waiting for previous versions to stop. It returns a Promise that immediately resolves to undefined. This is usually put into the install event handler as the final instruction. For example:

```
addEventListener("install",
        function (event) {
            console.log("install");

            event.waitUntil(
                async function () {
                        code that loads the cache etc
                        return skipWaiting();
                    }

                }());
        });
```

It doesn't stop the previous version from servicing pages that are already open, but any new pages will use the new version. It also causes the Service Worker to move to the active state and it fires the active event. If you want to take over the open pages you can use the Clients.claim method. This takes over all of the open pages at once. You have to be aware that the pages that you take over will have been created by the previous Service Worker. You can use Clients.claim anywhere that makes sense, but it is usual to put in the active event handler:

```
addEventListener('activate',
                    function(event) {
                        return self.clients.claim();
});
```

It also triggers a controllerchange event which gives you a chance to clean up.

The clients object is worth looking up as it has methods that allow you to interact with the current clients directly.

Finally, how do you remove a Service Worker?

The answer is that you first use the getRegistrations method to return a Promise which resolves to an array of ServiceWorkerRegistration objects:

```
var regs=await navigator.serviceWorker.getRegistrations();
```

Next you scan though the array to find the Service Worker you want to remove, either by scope or by state say. You then use the unregister method of that ServiceWorkerRegistration object.

For example to remove all Service Workers you would use:

```
async function remove() {
    var regs = await navigator.serviceWorker.getRegistrations();
    for (let reg of regs) {
        reg.unregister();
    }
}
```

Browsers also provide ways to manage Service Workers. For example, Chrome has an Application tab which can be used to monitor and stop Service Workers. You can also select different behaviors which are useful in testing. For example you can simulate offline working:

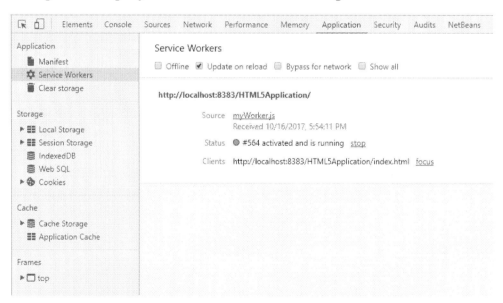

Also notice that you can examine and manage the cache.

The Future Of Service Workers

In this chapter we have only touched on the basic use of Service Workers. In addition to acting as a proxy for resource requests, there are also interfaces for implementing periodic synchronization and push notifications. In short, Service Workers offer opportunities that are difficult to realize any other way. Many think that modern JavaScript, HTML and CSS plus new APIs such as Service Workers and those that are related will allow the web to develop in new ways and make web apps as good as desktop apps. The only problem at the time of writing is that Microsoft's Edge browser is only just starting to implement the technology and until very recently Apple's Safari team had no intention of implementing it. Now it looks as if Safari will support it at some time in the future.

At the time of writing it is estimated that over 70% of users have a browser that supports Service Workers. Many large companies have decided that this is enough to make it worth the trouble to implement Service workers – Google, Twitter, FaceBook, Bloomberg and You Tube.

It does look as if Service Workers are the future of the web.

Summary

- New JavaScript APIs tend to use Promises and this means they are best used with async and await.

- The Fetch and Cache APIs are two good examples and these are fundamental to using the new Service Worker.

- The Fetch API is a modern implementation of the XMLHttpRequest and it can be used to download almost any file the browser has access to, and to send data to the server using Get or Post.

- The Fetch API uses Request and Response objects to specify the resource location and represent the response.

- The cache API is a replacement for appCache.

- The CacheStorage object stores a set of Cache objects each of which stores a set of key value pairs.

- A Service Worker is associated with a scope – a range of URLs – and once installed it is active whenever the browser loads a URL in the scope.

- The Service Worker intercepts all URLs in its scope via the Fetch event.

- The Service Worker can return a Response object which has been retrieved from a Cache object or it can construct a Response object from scratch. It acts as a proxy server and enables an app to function offline as well as online.

Index

162

Printed in Great Britain
by Amazon